Omward Bound

**How alternative woo-woo, a messed-up relationship
and an introverted horse
helped me become a kinder, happier person.**

J. Tanner Jones, Ph.D.

*To Naomi,
In Love and gratitude
for your role on my path,
Juliet*

Published by BookLocker.com, Inc., St. Petersburg, Florida, U.S.A.

Printed on acid-free paper.

BookLocker.com, Inc.
2017

First Edition

Disclaimer

This book details the author's personal experiences with and opinions about alternative healing and spirituality. The author is not a licensed counselor.

The author and publisher are providing this book and its contents on an "as is" basis and make no representations or warranties of any kind with respect to this book or its contents. The author and publisher disclaim all such representations and warranties, including for example warranties of merchantability and healing advice for a particular purpose. In addition, the author and publisher do not represent or warrant that the information accessible via this book is accurate, complete or current.

The statements made about products and services have not been evaluated by the U.S. government. Please consult with your own legal, accounting, medical, or other licensed professional regarding the suggestions and recommendations made in this book.

Except as specifically stated in this book, neither the author or publisher, nor any authors, contributors, or other representatives will be liable for damages arising out of or in connection with the use of this book. This is a comprehensive limitation of liability that applies to all damages of any kind, including (without limitation) compensatory; direct, indirect or consequential damages; loss of data, income or profit; loss of or damage to property and claims of third parties.

You understand that this book is not intended as a substitute for consultation with a licensed clinical counseling, medical, legal or accounting professional. Before you begin any change your lifestyle in any way, you will consult a licensed professional to ensure that you are doing what's best for your situation.

This book provides content related to alternative healing and spirituality topics. As such, use of this book implies your acceptance of this disclaimer.

Omward Bound

To the sea turtles off the coast of Maui.
Thanks for hanging with me.

Table of Contents

INTRODUCTION

On my first day as an official graduate student, a colorful professor, who wore an East Texas twang like a sheriff's badge of honor, began his lecture by telling us The Secret to achieving low limits of detection.

"It's not about making more and more sensitive detectors," he drawled. Then, lowering his voice to a conspiratorial tone and drawing us in for a closer listen, he continued. "It's all about lowering the background nise."

Background nise? Am I an idiot or did I miss that day in my undergraduate chemistry classes? What the hell is background nise? Oh! Noise! Background noise! Got it.

"You thank the stars go away in the daytime? No! They're still there. You just cayn't see them because of all the background nise. Take away the background nise, and I'll show you stars in the daytime."

It wasn't until many years later (19 to be precise) that the significance of his explanation hit me. I was a bit of a basket case at the time. I was stuck in yet another emotionally toxic relationship that would soon end in my fourth divorce before the age of 50. Despite an alphabet soup of degrees after my name and over a year of job hunting, I had been unable to find the right job. I had sacrificed most of my assets to my marriage and had no idea how I would survive on my own. I was so ashamed of my situation. I was desperately insecure, resentful, emotionally manipulative, judgmental – you name it.

I would like to say that this all was simply the result of the bad situation I found myself in, but if I were honest - also not my strong suit - I would have to admit that being unhappy and sometimes just plain mean was a persistent pattern. I had been prone to bouts of depression and hopelessness since my early teens. I am a survivor of numerous periods of simply wanting to die, but being unable to find the courage to actually succeed (one example of a situation in which fear of failure is actually a good thing).

I could take an instant dislike to someone whom I didn't even know. I would be standing in a line, or waiting at the doctor's office, and the most awful dialogue would be playing in my head about the people around me. I recently read a story in the paper about a woman who was waiting in line at a department store during the busy pre-Christmas season, when someone added her items to the cart of a friend just in front of the woman. "[Expletive] [Racial Epithet]!" she yelled. "When you're in this country, you go by OUR rules. Lean to speak English! Go back to where you came from!" Of course, a bystander captured the incident on video and posted it on social media, where it went viral.

After my initial disgust and rush to judgment, I thought to myself, "Don't be so hard on her. The only difference between her and you at one time is that she said it out loud."

I, on the other hand, carefully hid my "soul full of gunk," as the Grinch called it, from even my closest friends and my family. Except for the unemployment - they got to hear all about that. By all appearances, though, I was funny, smart, almost always smiling. I was the last person anyone would ever suspect of being depressed or seriously pissed off. But in retrospect, I was like a human wrecking ball with a big yellow smiley face painted on it, swinging from one partner, one job, one home to the next and leaving hurt, destruction and destroyed bridges behind me.

So what was wrong with me? Was I, as I hoped, a fundamentally good person, whose dark side just got the upper hand sometimes? Or was I, as I feared, a horrible, crazy person who just managed to put on a good act most of the time? Would I ever just be happy? Would I ever just...be?

Then I remembered the professor's words about stars during the day. "Maybe I'm like the stars in the daytime," I thought. "Maybe I have this light within me, trying its hardest to be seen, but it's buried under so much crap, so much hurt and anger and frustration from trying to live up to my unrealistic expectations – so much *nise* – that no one gets to see it. Maybe all I need to do is find a way to reduce the background noise."

Later still, I would find that Eckhart Tolle had already described something similar. In his book "The Power of Now," he writes about occasionally being approached by people who ask him, "I want what you have. Can you give it to me, or show me how to get it?" And he replies, "You have it already. You just can't feel it because your mind is making too much noise."

So, this is my story of personal noise reduction, discovered by exploring and embracing so-called alternative approaches that I had been taught my entire life to doubt, ridicule and avoid. I share some stories interspersed with what I view as significant steps along the way, in the hope that these may help and encourage others who wonder whether they're crazy and/or hopeless. These steps weren't revealed to me in their entirety before I began. At the time, I more or less stumbled upon them (or as I now believe, was guided, but if you're not there yet, just stick with stumbled).

Never in a million years could I have guessed where this path would lead. I'm happy to now be able to say I barely recognize in myself the basket case I described. I do still remember her – very vividly. But instead of viewing her with contempt and shame, I now embrace her warmly, in awe and admiration of her strength, and with forgiveness.

Bottom line: If you can have an open mind (like scientists like myself are actually supposed to have), and take a little leap of faith (like the church is constantly encouraging us to do), and not be afraid to look or feel like a bit of an idiot at times, you might be surprised. Ask yourself: "Why *can't* that be true?" "What's the worst that can happen?" "What was *my* experience of that?" "Was it helpful to *me*?"

Again, this is my path. Yours will be different. And as an attorney, I feel obligated – compelled, even – to include the following:

Legal disclaimer: All steps are intended as general guidance only and not as directives. Basic understanding of the use of internet search engines, tempered with rudimentary critical thinking skills, is assumed on behalf of the reader. Reader accepts responsibility for any and all undertakings, experiences and insights, whether brilliant or the stupidest idea ever in recorded history. Reader is advised that this book contains naughty language, and that editorial liberties have been taken with names, places and sequences of events to ensure privacy. Reader is further assured that the authors of any recommended books probably are not even aware of this author's existence, and have offered no compensation – seriously, none - for endorsements.

Chapter 1

Being Omless

Rat: "I'm too stressed. Too nervous. Too rushed.
I need peace in my life. I need calm."
Goat: "Try meditation."
Rat: (a few seconds later) "It didn't work."

~ From the comic strip "Pearls Before
Swine," by Stephan Pastis

Like Sedona, Arizona, with its vortices and portals, northern New Mexico is said to be a really spiritual place, brimming with lots of good energy. I felt absolutely none of that. Though I do remember vividly, even during this first visit, the feeling of familiarity. To this day, I feel my soul exhale whenever I step off a plane in the southwest.

Driving to my job interview, the snow-capped Sandia and Sangre de Christo mountains overlooking the vast moonscape calmed my nerves. As I navigated the winding, uphill road, my attention inescapably reverted to worst-case interview scenarios.

"So, why do you want to work here?" the stern-faced interviewer asks while peering at me over the top of reading glasses perched on the end of her nose.

"Oh, I don't know really," I say as calmly as I could, trying to hide the fact that I had just discovered my fly is open. "Maybe I don't want to at all, but as long as I do have to work, I might as well enjoy beautiful scenery and be able to show up at work wearing jeans and hiking boots and head out for a lunchtime hike. Or maybe, as a patent

attorney, it would be cool to, oh, I don't know, say, patent actual inventions? Maybe I'm tired of trying to squeeze blood out of the non-inventive turnips of patent applications that I'm ordered to pursue to the death, despite numerous rejections from the patent office that are sometimes so soul-crushing, that if they came from the opposite sex, would make me wholeheartedly embrace a life of celibacy?"

"I see. And what would you say are your biggest weaknesses?"

"Well, for starters, when I'm asked canned questions by people who are clearly phoning it in, I have a hard time being patient and not having a look on my face as clear as a flashing neon sign saying 'What, are you stupid?' But o.k., I'll play along. Golly. Gosh. Well, I am kind of a perfectionist. And some say I'm just too darn nice of a person sometimes."

"O.k. And where do you see yourself in five years?"

"How the hell would I know? I've never even been able to predict where and with whom I'll be spending my next Christmas."

Oh well. If all else fails, this would at least be the most beautiful drive to a job interview I've ever had.

But miraculously, it didn't fail. I managed to keep a lid on my inner voices and outer facial expressions, and so I began my new job a few months later, vowing to continue to keep that lid firmly in place.

A notice arrived in my inbox one day about free lunchtime classes being offered for employees. One was entitled "How to Meditate." I paused just as I was about to hit delete. *Meditation? Maybe that would help me with keeping the lid in place.* I pictured myself sitting in

6

meetings, calm and serene, unflappable despite being surrounded by heated disagreements.

I'd never really thought about meditation, except for hippies and people from India. The Dalai Lama meditates, and he seems pretty happy. But he probably learned meditation before he was potty-trained, so he doesn't count. Was it on the list of things for which the Catholic Church said I would go to hell? Well, if it was, that ship has sailed anyway. Divorce and remarriage had secured my place in that particular hand basket. An hour at lunchtime didn't seem too scary. I signed up.

About thirty people filled the room, by the looks of them mostly science types whose clothing tended more toward function than form. Our instructor was a bit different than I had imagined. No flowery flowing dress, no jewelry in the shape of a peace sign or dangling crystal earrings, no sensible shoes. No cushions on the floor, either. We sat on regular folding chairs, side by side, as if attending a lecture.

"I began meditating about ten years ago, like many of you here today, and just never stopped. You just have to commit to doing it," she said. "Don't worry about 'doing it right,' or meditating as 'deep as a Buddhist monk,'" she said, accentuating her points with bunny-ear finger motions. "Just decide that you are worth 5 minutes, or 15 minutes, or 30 minutes just for yourself, and notice what happens."

She asked us to sit quietly until a word came to us that we would like to use as our anchor. Maybe it would be "love" or "peace" - whatever came to mind and felt right would be o.k. She then instructed us to breathe in, focusing our attention on our breath, and as we breathe out, to repeat our anchor word silently to ourselves. We would do this for 15 minutes.

Fifteen minutes. Piece of cake. Mmmm, cake. Oh, that sounded like Homer Simpson: Do-nut... Donuts are good too. My favorites are the ones with white frosting. Sprinkles are optional. People use a lot of lawn sprinklers around here. Maybe that's why there's more grass than I thought there'd be. Not a lot, but more than in Arizona. Not Scottsdale - the rest of Arizona. Arizona is beautiful. Much more beautiful than I had envisioned. I thought it would be like the Sahara, with rolling sand dunes as far as the eye could see. I loved the big saguaro cactuses. Cacti? Wait, what is the plural of cactus? Cactuses? "You say cactusus, I say cacti..." And the roadrunners. There are roadrunners here too. But they're not three feet tall and purple and they don't go "meep meep!" Oh crap – you're supposed to be meditating. Focus, stupid!!! What should your word be? I dunno. How about just go with Love? O.k. Love. Loooooooove.

Second breath.

Dang. This was hard. Should be easy. What's my problem? What am I doing here? I'm a scientist, not some hippie-dippy meditator. O.k., fine, maybe I'm technically a lawyer now, but I'm a scientist at heart. I want to believe in this kind of thing, but honestly, my belief system is still pretty much intact since Catholic school. And from the scientific method. Oh well, I'm here now. Might as well play along.

Third breath.

I relaxed a bit and started to get over feeling self-conscious and acutely aware that I was sitting in a slightly dilapidated building with thirty strangers. *O.k... I think I can do this. Love. Loooooooove. Luhhhv. Love somebody. Love makes the world go round. Like a merry-go-round. Do do do do do do do do do do. Hey! Hey!! HEY!!! You're doing it again! Pay attention!!!*

Fourth breath.

As the 15 minutes neared an end, I felt someone softly touching my forehead with the back of their hand, as if to check whether I had a fever.

That was nice. It must be the instructor – everyone else was sitting still. But why would she do that? Was I looking flushed? Was something there that needed brushing away that simply couldn't wait another few minutes? I quickly opened my eyes, keeping my head lowered as I glanced furtively around the room.

The instructor sat at the front of the room, in meditation with the rest of us. It couldn't have been her. I glanced quickly at the people on either side of me. They sat quietly with eyes closed as well.

Strange.

That convinced me, though. I decided to do as the instructor had advised, and just do it. I committed to meditating every day. I never really considered myself "a meditator" though, because I wasn't sure whether I was doing it right. I still got awfully distracted at times. I definitely wasn't having profound insights or visions. I wanted to learn more, but how? Who would be able to teach me?

Of course - Buddhists! Weren't Buddhists really good at meditating? Maybe they would let me hang out with them for a while to learn how to meditate better. How would I find them, though? Of course – Google! I searched "Buddhist meditation" along with my town, and was shocked when a local group popped up as the first hit. Who knew there were Buddhists walking among us? And I was welcome to join them at their next Wednesday evening meditation.

I gathered my courage, and drove to the address. It was an ordinary ranch home in an ordinary subdivision. I rang the bell, and waited, envisioning the door being answered by a small Asian guy wearing a robe. Instead, I was greeted by a rather large, very Caucasian person.

"Oh…," I stammered. "I must have the wrong address."

"Are you here for meditation?" he asked.

"Uh, yes."

"Then you've come to the right place. Take off your shoes and come in. And next time, you don't need to ring the bell. You can just come right in."

I entered what seemed like a normal living room, and was greeted by several others. None wore robes, and all were Caucasian. There was no incense, no sitar music. In an adjacent room, however, a statue of the Buddha on an altar filled on one wall, and along the other walls were cushions and chairs.

I received a brief set of instructions before we began. Bow before entering the meditation space, and then bow to the Buddha, but realize that you're not really worshipping Buddha, because the Buddha actually represents myself. *Uh-huh.* I nodded as if I understood. Sit in a chair, on a cushion, or kneel – whichever is most comfortable. When the bell is rung, begin. When it is rung 30 minutes later, stop. When your thoughts wander, just observe them and bring your attention back to your breathing. There will be two 30-minute meditations.

I sat down on the floor, and closed my eyes when the bell sounded. Thirty minutes later – or maybe three hours, not quite sure – the bell sounded again. My feet had turned into blocks of concrete from not having sat cross-legged for so long since kindergarten. But I had done it. Whew!

In the end, I learned there really is no trick to meditation - I actually had been doing it correctly. Guess that giant sports equipment manufacturer had it right after all. You just have to do it.

As I would come to learn, nothing is too strange in meditation. Tingling in my hands; pressure in my forehead that could be so intense as to be uncomfortable; the feeling of my heart expanding into infinity; feeling like I could float away like a balloon yet being somehow tethered to the ground; interpretations of dreams that before had completely puzzled me; sudden insights. Anything is possible.

But did I suddenly become the serene, unflappable person I had envisioned? No. Nor could I, to my disappointment, suddenly sense that wonderful energy lurking in all those New Mexico "vortices." But I did notice that when I was working on something, especially something pretty boring, I would become aware of my thoughts wandering, and was able to gently steer them back to what I was doing. When I was speaking with someone, I was better able to really focus on what they were saying, instead of what I was going to say in response. If I found myself waiting in line or stuck in traffic, I would just view it as an opportunity to practice awareness of my thoughts and surroundings, and suddenly, I didn't mind so much having to wait.

Many years later, I would look around the room at the group of co-workers who had answered my invitation to learn meditation. "I learned to meditate at my job, like many of you here today, and just never stopped," I began. "You just have to commit to doing it."

MORAL OF THE STORY ONE: PRACTICE MEDITATION

I can already hear some of you groaning about this one. Meditation, mindfulness – they're everywhere these days, being touted as a cure to all that ails. However, of all the wacked-out alternative stuff I would eventually try and that would come and go, this is The Best thing I've ever done. I now view it as a fundamental skill - a building block, if you will – for so many of the other steps I talk about in this book.

I could recite the many physiological and psychological benefits of meditation. I could tell you that it will make you calmer and generally feel better. It does. But I believe the real reason to learn to meditate is this:

In order to listen, we have to shut up.

Many of us have been taught to pray, and for those so inclined, it's a wonderful practice. But prayer is about talking. And what good is talking if we never stop to listen to the answer? How annoying is it to hear someone go on and on and on about something, leaving you to wonder whether duct tape ever really is an acceptable solution? (The answer, by the way, is "usually no, but it depends.") Ever think God must feel the same way?

Me: "Please, Lord, help me to find a new place to live."
God: "Well, I think if you…"
Me: "Any place right now. I just need to be able to have my pets with me."
God: "Yes, I agree, and I want to suggest…"
Me: "I'll do anything…just show me the way."
God: "Well, as I've been trying to tell you, what's most important right now is…"
Me: "Our Father, who art in heaven…"

God: "Yes. It's me, and I am. Now, as I was saying…"
Me: "Hail Mary, full of grace…"
God: "Oh, honest to me. I give up."

That's where meditation comes in. Meditation is the first step toward noise reduction.

I hear so many people say they can't meditate. "I can't sit still for so long and do nothing. I get bored," are the most common reasons.

"Ten breaths," I answer. "Just start with ten breaths. If that's not possible, then don't try to meditate. Allow yourself the luxury of just being, with no demands, no expectations. Just sit quietly for a few minutes, and build from there."

Here's some additional recommendations:

1. Decide on a time of day that works, and make it a part of your daily routine. My best time is after dinner. Other people say they would fall asleep if they tried to meditate after dinner, and prefer to do it first thing in the morning. Whatever works best is fine.

2. Decide on a place and a position. Just make sure your spine is upright, yet relaxed. Don't let anyone tell you that sitting in a chair is cheating, and that real meditation is done in the lotus position. That's just meditation snobbery. I cannot sit on the floor cross-legged without my feet falling asleep, and then that's all I can think about. So I started in a chair, and now I kneel while using a "meditation bench" that I place behind my knees for support. If you do sit, try to

place your feet flat on the floor. Your hands can either rest on your thighs (facing up or down), or you can place the back of one hand in the palm of the other, with your thumbnails softly touching.

3. Try several different forms of meditation, and see what works best for you. There are lots of books, videos and free downloads available, so I won't get into the details here. You can try guided meditations, walking meditations (such as labyrinths), or the classic "simply focus on your breath" (which, as you read earlier, is both very simple and very challenging).

4. Set a timer. Preferably with a nice, soft sound. When you begin to get into "a meditative state," as I call it, sudden sounds can startle you, and will seem as if they go right through you. You might not even be aware you're in such a state until you hear a sound. If it makes you jump, or sounds louder than it is, your brain is in an altered state, and you're having a good meditation.

5. Speaking of which, there will be good meditations and not-so-good ones. Some days you'll experience something amazing, and other days your thoughts will be non-stop and scattered all over the place. Don't worry about it. Just accept that's the best you can do right now, and give yourself credit for trying. Tomorrow's meditation may be better.

Chapter 2

It's Pronounced "Ray-Key"

Scooter: "Can I join you?"
Janice: "For sure! Just hang your aura by the door and come on in. I think that first hook is free."
~ From *The Muppet Show*

In a comic book world full of superheroes and villains, my hero would be Dr. Denial, Grand Master of Ignoring the Obvious. His sidekick would be Captain Cliché, who would chime in with aptly timed, worn-out platitudes that fall just short of making me feel better, and to which I never really know how to respond. Just like me, Dr. Denial has no insecurities, no major problems. Life wasn't stressful. I woke up in the mornings looking forward to going to work. I loved my job. I loved my husband, loved the beautiful area in which I lived, loved volunteering at the local animal shelter. No, no, no, that wasn't difficult or depressing or frustrating at all. Life was good!

That little breakdown, sobbing hysterically to my husband that our other house hadn't sold as planned, and I didn't know how to make my salary stretch to cover two mortgages?

"*No problem,*" *Dr. Denial reassured. "That's just built up tension that you needed to get out of your system.*"

"*There, there,*" *Captain Cliché chimes in, "Everything will be fine.*"

The fact that my husband had agreed before moving that the only way we could make it work was if we were both earning, and yet he remained gainfully unemployed?

"*No, you're not angry or resentful about that. It's not that he can't find a job,*" Dr. Denial explains patiently. "*The paperwork for his license is just taking longer than we thought. That's just bad luck.*"

Cue Captain Cliché: "*And bad things happen to good people sometimes.*"

The fact that our love life had been virtually non-existent since our marriage three years earlier?

"*But you're best friends,*" Dr. D reassures. "*That's what's really important.*"

Yes, we are. Thanks Doc! You always know the right thing to say!

In this week's episode of *Dr. Denial's Spiritual Quest*, I find myself browsing in the metaphysical section of a bookstore. As I turned to walk away, a book falls onto the floor. It's about something called Reiki. As the inside cover explained, pronounced "ray-kee."

"Ding!" The light bulb above my head suddenly appears. "So *that's* how you spell that!"

My mind flashed back to a conversation I'd had a year or so earlier. An intern in a corporate legal department, I sat in the office of my boss' boss' boss. She was an intimidating woman – a tough-as-nails attorney cloaked in a drippingly sweet, southern accent, who intimidated even senior management let alone a lowly intern. She showed me a small vial with a dark purple liquid inside.

"Ah have no idea what's in there, but ah tell people it's a voodoo potion. They never know whether to believe me or not," she said, laughing.

"Well, whatever works," I replied. *Thanks again, Captain!*

"Ah sometimes sit with mah girlfriends, and we like to try distance ray-key on our husbands. Then we ask them later, 'hey, did y'all notice anything around 4 o'clock or so?'" I laughed and nodded, not wanting to admit that I had no idea what in the hell ray-key is.

I scanned the book. A Japanese healing method, I read. A way of sending good vibes via your hands, which allows the healer to cure, in principle, everything under the sun. Advanced students learn the use of secret symbols. There's the "power symbol," that allows you to magnify your own power. There's the "distance healing symbol," that allows you to send energy anywhere in the world. Apparently anyone could learn it. All you had to do was take a weekend class, and get certified by someone who was already a Reiki Master. I wanted to learn!

But wait…shouldn't I at least experience it first?

Fast forward to a week later. I'm driving along a remote road, holding a sheet of paper scribbled with directions, on the steering wheel in front of me. The thought vaguely occurs to me that this may not be the smartest thing I've ever done. No one knew where I was going.

What if the Reiki Master is an ax murderer? What if he's a smart, evil ax murderer and hypnotized me into becoming an ax murdering apprentice? What if he's just a creepy pervert? "Now relax…it's critical to the flow of energy that I place both hands over your boobs and hold them there. Oooh…I'm sensing some energetic imbalance in your lady parts. Now just hold still while I take care of that."

"That's ridiculous," Dr. Denial says reassuringly. "Healers are good people. Otherwise they wouldn't be healers, would they?"

"Of course," chimes in Captain Cliché. "Worrying won't pay the rent now, will it?"

No, it won't. You know what else it won't pay? Two stupid mortgages.

If the man who answered the door was an ax murderer, he would be really good at flying under the radar. Stephen had longish gray hair, and incredibly kind eyes. He was quiet, and a bit serious. Put a headband on him, and he could have been an Indian chief. He showed me into a typical cozy southwest-style living room, with tile floors, stucco walls and brightly colored area rugs. He introduced me to a tall, smiling woman, and asked if it was o.k. for his girlfriend to join us, as she was in the process of learning Reiki.

"Sure," I said.

"See?" Dr. Denial says. "Ax murderers don't typically invite girlfriends along."

Oh, please, Dr. D. The girlfriends are usually the last to know.

We all sat down, and Stephen explained the process. I would lay on the massage table set up in the middle of the room. Clothes stayed on, and they would cover me with a blanket to make sure I stayed warm. They would both place their hands on me, in various positions. If I didn't feel their hands, it was because they were holding them above some part of my body that they did not want to touch.

"What will I feel?" I asked.

"Maybe heat, maybe tingling," he explained. "Maybe you don't notice much of anything, except a sense of relaxation. Or it could be days later that you notice things. Everyone's different. Every treatment is different." He paused briefly to let this sink in. "Ready?"

I nodded, climbed onto the table, and closed my eyes.

It took only a few minutes before I noticed their warm hands on my feet and knees through the blanket. Then after a few more minutes they got REALLY warm - warmer than one would normally expect hands could be.

Oh my gosh, I'm so gullible. Of course, they're holding hot pads in their hands!

I opened my eyes to see whether this was indeed the case.

"You o.k.?" Stephen asked.

"Yeah, yeah...fine...it's just...never mind." There were no hot pads. No heated wraps. Just hands. I closed my eyes again.

As their hand positions progressed upward toward my chest, I felt the hands disappear, but not the heat. That's when I noticed the trembling inside - like tiny bubbles of champagne running in rivulets underneath my skin. It was a strange, wonderful feeling.

After what seemed like only a few minutes, the treatment was over. I glanced at the clock. An hour had gone by in what seemed like just a short time. Stephen and Carol helped me to sit up and walked me over to the couch.

"Well?" he asked, looking at me intently. "How do you feel now?"

I explained about the champagne bubbles, which by now had progressed to visible shakiness. "It's not unpleasant, but just strange."

He asked Carol to get me some tea, and asked if I would like to try a few drops of Rescue Remedy.

Ah...Here it comes. Now that I'm all relaxed, they're going to slip me the drugs.

She returned, and showed me a tiny bottle with a dropper. "It's an herbal remedy," she explained. "We use it on our pets and on ourselves. It just calms and relaxes. Want to try?"

"Really, dear," Dr. Denial says. *"Think about it. If someone were trying to drug you and take advantage of you, would they go through all the trouble of emptying a bottle of an herbal remedy, replacing the contents with poison, and then make such a show of explaining it to you? Don't be so silly."*

"And besides," chimes in The Captain, *"what doesn't kill you only makes you stronger."*

What doesn't what?! Poor choice of words, Captain. Poor choice of words.

As I drank the tea, the trembling stopped. There was only relaxation.

Stephen and Carol explained that I may notice some strange things in the coming days. It was like some sort of surreal pharmaceutical commercial: *Recipients of Reiki may experience a feeling of not being fully present for a time after treatment. Temporary worsening of symptoms may occur. Side effects may include bizarre dreams, sudden onset tingling or warmth in the hands and/or fingers, and the ability to see spirits.*

Sadly, I experienced none of those.

"Pfft. Not that you wanted to anyway," Dr. D. snorted *indignantly.*

Arriving home, and back in my disguise as a buttoned-up patent attorney returning home from work, I walked into the door, and exchanged a quick kiss with my husband. My dogs scrambled to greet me, having difficulty until they reach surer footing on the carpet and thus a suitable launching pad to nearly bowl me over. I greeted them with equal enthusiasm, knowing that I was encouraging bad behavior, but happy that they were so happy.

"How was your day?" my husband asked.

Uh, well, interestingly…you see, I…oh screw it.

"Fine. Uneventful."

"See? No problems," Dr. D. and the Captain reassure me. *"Nothing at all to worry about here."*

No, nothing indeed.

MORAL OF THE STORY TWO:
LEARN ABOUT ENERGY WORK

Why on earth would I suggest you learn about energy work? Because, as I have learned, and am oh-so-slowly beginning to understand, everything is energy. Literally everything. Einstein had it right: On the one side of the equation is energy. On the other side is everything else.

I believe that, like meditation, being able to "work with energy" is another fundamental building block. Understanding energy, in the sense of how healers refer to it, will help you see so many things in an entirely different light. And, it will empower you to begin to heal yourself.

Being a skeptic, I struggled with energy healing. I thought it was all just people's imagination, or the result of the power of suggestion. But even I couldn't deny my experience. And so, as I encourage anyone to do, I did a lot of reading and research. What I found was that many aspects of Reiki have been proven by traditional scientific methods. For example, the energy emanating from practitioners' hands has been imaged, and found to occur in the range of low-micron wavelengths. Some mainstream medical establishments are allowing Reiki practitioners to offer treatments. Most importantly, though, my own experiences continue to surprise and convince me.

I now see the human energy field as common sense. As something so forehead-smackingly logical that it's not even a question of belief.

Think about it: According to Physics 101, what happens when you run electrical current through a conductor? For those of you who sucked at physics as badly as I did, the answer is that you create a magnetic field. What are our bodies, if not an electrical current in a conductor? Our heart generates its own electrical impulses. Our nervous system conducts electrical impulses. No one would dispute that we can see these things on EKG's and EEG's; we are therefore electrical beings. We also are composed primarily of water. As anyone who has ever accidentally touched an electrical fence while sticking a hand in a horse's water trough while her horse was enjoying a drink (ahem...) can attest, human beings (and horses) are conductive.

The energetic/magnetic/electric field surrounding our bodies is what energy workers refer to as our aura. It's also been detected by scientific instruments, and by Kirlian photography. Under the right conditions, even I can now see it. It's great entertainment during boring meetings.

Human beings can learn to sense and to interact with this field. The Bible contains stories of laying on of the hands to heal. Maybe we can't be as good at it as Jesus was, but we can learn. (Seriously, if I can, anyone can.)

To get a sense of what I'm talking about, try this: Rub your hands together. Tap with your finger on the palm of each hand. Now shake them out and wiggle your fingers. Hold your hands about a foot apart, palms facing each other. Now slowly move them toward each other until you feel something. It may be pressure, or tingling, or heat. Move them apart and closer together again to feel the difference. That is the energy we're talking about. It's that subtle. With practice, we can increase our ability to sense this energy, to build it, and to direct it. And the less "noisy" we are, the better we are able to do so (hence, Moral of the Story One).

There are many different modalities of energy work: Reiki, polarity work, pranic healing, healing touch, and T-touch are just a few. Each modality, in turn, may have many different schools, or variants. The important thing is to find what makes sense to you, what works for you, and an instructor with whom you feel comfortable. This comes down to trial and error, and ultimately common sense and judgment.

I chose to explore Reiki, in particular, the more traditional "Eastern" Reiki (as opposed to "Western" Reiki that's more often taught in the U.S.). "The Reiki Sourcebook," as well as other books by my down-to-earth and wonderfully funny teacher Frans Stiene, opened my eyes to a Reiki practice that resonated with me. I love the strong emphasis on meditation and on self-healing. However, I am in no way suggesting that this is right for everyone, or the only right approach.

Don't be afraid to ask a lot of questions, because yes, there are a lot of less-than-honorable practitioners. There also are those who are not necessarily dishonest, but whom I believe are a little too focused on self-promotion and making money.

What are some red flags when considering whether to take a course or work with an instructor?

In my opinion:
1. Cramming too much into too short of a time. For example, in Reiki, promising that you can become a "Master" (i.e., be "certified" in Levels I, II and III) in one weekend (or a similarly short time).
2. Excessively high cost. I'm talking thousands of dollars to achieve a certain level.
3. Claiming their method is the only true way, or better than any other approach, or who show a lack of respect for other modalities.

4. Making students feel dependent upon the instructor, for example, by teaching that the method "won't work unless they get periodic infusions of energy," coincidentally from that same instructor. The goal of a good instructor should be to eventually bring students to the point where they no longer need the instructor (though they may enjoy continuing to receive instruction).
5. Beware of anyone who refers to himself as a Reiki "Grand Master." Just make sure you ask what, exactly, makes this person so "Grand" that the title "Master" doesn't quite cut it.

The good news is, there is generally little risk involved in doing energy work. For the most part, the worst that can happen is, well, nothing. Whereas you may be out some time and money, in general, there is nothing seriously bad that will happen to you. So, be open, be skeptical, and as Captain Cliché might say, *"Enjoy the journey."*

Chapter 3

People with Access to Information I Don't Have

> *If there was a car crash blocks away, that window washer could likely see it. That doesn't mean he's God... or even smarter than we are. But from where he's sitting... he can see a little further down the road.*
> ~ From the movie "The Mothman Prophecies"

It always amazes me how members of secret groups somehow manage to find each other. Signals, phrases, a look, a sense...who knows how people who feel they can't openly talk about what they would like to talk about if they only knew they had "it" in common, actually manage to figure out that they do, indeed, have "it" in common without actually talking about "it" in the first place?

Sometimes I'll be sitting with a group of friends, and think to myself how odd and wonderful it is to have just mentioned the words "spirit guide," "past life," and "energy clearing" all in the same sentence and with the same tone of normalcy that one would use when discussing the final season of American Idol. And yet, if I would run into these people on the street, never in a million years would I think that they would be one of us. They all look so ... normal.

Hmm...so how many more are out there that I don't know about? Shouldn't we have a secret sign or symbol? The Masons have their rings. Same-sex oriented people have the rainbow. Something discrete, cryptic, yet fashionable... Just think how much easier that would make things? You get into a fender bender with someone, and as you're exchanging your insurance information, you say, "Excuse me, but I see by the lightening rod tattooed on the inside of your left thumb that you're a light worker. Well, then I don't need to tell you that there are no accidents! I guess we were supposed to meet today. I suppose that's what you get when you ignore the signs – the universe will find a way to make it happen."

"Ain't that the truth," she says, before hugging goodbye and promising to send healing energy to the situation.

I don't remember how my manager, Marnie, and I figured out it was safe to talk about spiritual stuff, but fortunately we had, because I was seriously confused about something I was reading.

"Heaven," the well-known psychic wrote, "is right here. All around us. It just vibrates at a different frequency, so we can't see it. Which is why it can co-exist in the same space."

Really? Hmm. Well, that explains the whole "heaven on earth" concept.

I continued reading. "And it's about three feet off the ground. That's why ghosts often seem to float above the ground."

Aw, dammit. You had me there for a while, but now you lost me. Three feet? Really? Why three feet? What if the ghosts trip and fall? Do they fall to a height of three feet above us, or come crashing down to our level? They weren't three feet above the ground in Beetlejuice. Now Casper, he floated. But he was more than three feet high. Actually, that was more like flying, not floating.

I asked Marnie about it the next day, as we drove to an off-site meeting.

"I dunno..." she said skeptically when asked about the three feet rule. "The ghost in my apartment wasn't three feet off the ground. Although, I did see him walk up an invisible staircase once. But on a similar topic," she continued, giving me a simultaneous sideways glance to gauge my reaction, "I'm thinking of going to see a psychic." She said the last word in a hushed, conspiratorial voice, her eyes darting from side to side.

"Do you have one in mind?" I asked.

"I do. His name is Thomas," she said, as she circled through the parking lot looking in vain for a space.

"Like the train?"

"Why yes, as a matter of fact. He seems authentic," she said, braking for a space that seemed empty, but was concealing a Mini.

"How do you know?"

"Well, he has stories on his website about how he just knew things growing up. He seems like a nice boy-next-door type." She pulled into a space near the front door having a sign that read, "15 minute time limit. Flashers must be on." She added, "And his office is close by work."

"Oh, well then," I said with a tone of mock confidence. "Works for me. I'm in. But aren't we going to be in our meeting longer than 15 minutes?"

"I don't think they'll even bother to check," she said, hitting the button to start the flashers.

Best. Manager. Ever.

And she was right. Four hours later, there sat her car, flashers still bravely blinking on in the falling dusk.

Driving to our appointment with Thomas later that week, I felt a long-forgotten rush. A sense that I was doing something kind of exciting and naughty.

Maybe this is what people get out of shoplifting or having an affair or taking drugs, but without the risk of getting arrested, divorced or fired.

28

Thomas' office was about as aligned with my expectations as was the Buddhist meditation group. Once again, there was no incense or sitar music. It was also well-lit. And the receptionist, who invited us to have a seat, had no mysterious Russian accent.

Maybe this is just a front, in case they're ever investigated.

If it was, the charade continued flawlessly in Thomas' office. Instead of a curtain made of beads, I entered through an actual door, complete with a door handle. As I closed it behind me, I found him sitting not at a small table with a long table cloth to hide what's underneath and a giant, opaque crystal ball on top, but behind a desk with a computer. If Marnie hadn't just exited the same room, I would have assumed I had mistakenly entered an accountant's office, and stammered an embarrassed apology before beating a hasty retreat.

"Welcome," he said, extending his hand with a smile.

I studied his face as I took his hand. He was a large, teddy-bear of a man, and like me, looked to be flirting with 40. Behind his wire-rimmed glasses, his eyes were kind. He invited me to sit with a wave of his arm. Apparently not being disposed toward chit-chat, he got right down to business.

"I like to tape my sessions, to give you to take with you," he said, unwrapping a pack of cassette tapes and popping one into a recorder. "Sometimes people remember things later, when they listen to it again. So, what would you like to know?"

Whether you're for real or whether this is the most colossally naïve thing I've ever done.

"Uh...well...," I stammered, "I'm just curious I suppose. About who is with me." Wanting to sound cooler than I was, I added nonchalantly, "You know, my guides."

He was silent for a moment, his gaze focused behind me and to my right. His eyes moved back and forth as if he were scanning a crowd, looking for a familiar face. I resisted the urge to turn and look for myself, and instead continued to watch him.

"It's so beautiful what I see," he said. "There are animals all around you. All different kinds of animals."

"Cool!"

"There are people too – a man and a woman – but way more animals. Deer. All kinds. I'm seeing two dogs. I'm not familiar with dog breeds. One looks like a golden retriever, or something like that. Kind of long fur. Big. The other looks, I don't know, like a beagle? Brown and white. Spotted or dots or something. Good size, but smaller than the other."

A beagle?! I've certainly never owned a beagle.

I searched my memory, recalling the dogs I'd had growing up and who were long since gone. None fit the description. "You're sure it's not a Rottweiler, or Doberman-like?" I asked, hoping that my beloved Rottie was still with me.

"No," he said, shaking his head. "Those are breeds I'm actually familiar with, and that's not what I'm seeing."

I shook my head, and said I didn't know.

"The man seems to be your father."

"He passed away last year," I offered. *Shhhh! Don't tell him that! See if he knows! Oh well, too late.* "How's he doing?"

"Not too well."

Good. Glad to hear it.

"Was there something about writing? Maybe something he gave you? Something you found?"

Something he gave me? The man gave me nothing. And don't think I don't know what you're doing – throwing vague things against the wall to see what sticks. If it wouldn't have been my father, you would have guessed my grandfather. And what father doesn't give some kind of writing to his daughter, even a crappy birthday card. Well, except for mine. Nice try.

I forced myself to search my memory, and again shook my head.

"Well, think about it. There's something to do with writing. Maybe something will turn up. In any event, he's struggling. He's indicating he's sorry."

Right. Whatever.

"Your mother seems to be there too. But she's not standing near him. That tells me either that their work is done, or that they didn't get along very well and they're still working through it."

"Well, that would be putting it mildly," I said, laughing. "I can imagine she still wants nothing to do with him."

He paused, again scanning the area off to one side of me back and forth with his eyes. "Do you have any moves planned?" he asked.

"No," I said, shaking my head. I was starting to feel sorry for him. "In fact, I'll be happy if I never have to move again."

"Nope. Sorry. You're not done yet. What's with I...? Illinois? Idaho?

I stared blankly.

On the way back to the office, Marnie and I were a bit quiet. "I don't know," I said. "I wanted to believe what he was saying, because, hey, who wouldn't want to hear they have the San Diego Zoo surrounding them? But let's face it, a lot of it just didn't ring true. Like that part about my father. Who was a complete waste of perfectly good carbon, by the way. And since you ask..."

"I didn't."

"But since you did," I continued. "I only have a few memories of him, you know, and none of them good. Still, in a last-ditch effort to take the high road, I, being the good little girl that I am, actually wrote him a letter a few years back. It wasn't mean or accusatory or anything. I just told him where I was living, that I was in graduate school, that kind of thing. I gave him my address. I never heard back from him. Screw it. It was a stupid thing to do, but at least writing it gave me some closure." My voice trailed off.

Was there something about writing? He's struggling...He's indicating he's sorry... No, it couldn't be. And anyway, Thomas asked if I had received any writing from him, not the other way around. If he was any good, wouldn't he have known that I was the one who'd written the letter?

That evening, as I entered my home, I heard the familiar scrambling of paws on the wood floor as my dogs rushed to greet me. I bent down to rub and kiss the furry heads whose very life seemed to depend on properly greeting me, laughing as they nearly knocked me over. My giant boy, my Leonberger, with his gold and sable fur and black mask, and my girl, with her tan and white markings and light beige flecks the only outward expression of her Saint Bernard lineage.

It wasn't until I lay in bed that it hit me.

I'm not familiar with dog breeds. One looks like a golden retriever, or something like that. Kind of long fur. Big. The other looks, I don't know, like a beagle. Brown and white. Spotted or dots or something. Good size, but smaller than the other.

It wasn't a golden retriever and a beagle Thomas was seeing. Nor were they long gone. They were very much alive and lay next to my bed breathing softly.

MORAL OF THE STORY THREE:
ESTABLISH A RELATIONSHIP WITH YOUR GUIDES

If I haven't lost you with the first two steps, I'll probably lose you here. All I can say is 1) I wouldn't blame you, and 2) trust me (says the lawyer).

Am I suggesting you start visiting psychics on a regular basis? No, but if you want to, use the same skepticism, openness and judgment that you would use in exploring anything else. What I'm suggesting is that you, in effect, become your own psychic.

But while we're on the subject, let me say that I really dislike the term "psychic," simply because of all the negative associations. I prefer to use the term "people with access to information that I don't have." However, since this phrase is a bit unwieldy, I will use the term "psychic," but with great respect for the gifted and conscientious ones out there.

Having been raised Catholic, the idea of being surrounded by unseen beings was not new. However, these were in the form of angels. For whatever reason, these type of unseen beings were perfectly acceptable, whereas the idea of spirit guides was far-fetched New Age voodoo. Now, however, I have to move the concept of spirit guides from the "New Age voodoo" category to the "forehead-smackingly obvious" category, again, simply because of my experiences.

As with Reiki, my first step was to read more about the subject. I love reading books by people who, like myself, were trained in the traditional sciences and had to overcome their own disbelief. Two books in particular had a profound impact on me. The first was "Many Lives, Many Masters," by Brian L. Weiss. The second was "Journey of

Souls," by Michael Newton, Ph.D. However, the person who was able to explain the concept most simply and clearly to me was my friend Diana Rankin, who is also a writer, teacher and psychic medium from whom I've learned such a great deal. I'll attempt my own explanation here, but I also refer you to her books, website and videos.

First of all, we are not alone. And by that I don't mean that there are aliens watching us (my jury is still out on that one), but that we all have our own personal support staff. We are part of a team, and that team's sole purpose is to support us during our lifetime.

We chose and assembled this team before we were born, while still in spirit form. Together, we decided upon what we want to learn, and how we will go about it. Since this is such a huge undertaking, and the world, or "Earth plane" as some refer to it, is a pretty rough place, we have a lot of members on the team. Some are in the forefront, others sit in the back of the classroom and only raise their hand when they have something really important to say. One thing to remember, though, is that you and your team really are in this together. They are learning from you as much as you are learning from them. It's almost as if they're pushing you ahead and saying, "O.k.– go get 'em! And by the way, let us know how it works out!"

To use an analogy: Imagine you're a lawyer, about to try an important case. You've worked as part of a team, preparing every angle of the case. Now it's time for you to go in front of the judge and jury, and it's all on you. Everyone pats you on the back and sends you into the court room. Now imagine your entire team keeps giving you advice during the trial. They even talk over one another as they try to make their points. That wouldn't work very well, would it? You'd be so overwhelmed with advice that you wouldn't know what to do. So instead, you pick one person – your most trusted – to sit at the table with you as co-counsel. Occasionally you lean over and confer. Your co-counsel, in turn, may turn around and consult with your team, but in the end, their advice all gets filtered through him. He gives his perspective, and then the final decision as to which course of action to follow is yours.

The co-counsel is your main spirit guide, or "communicator guide." He (or she, but since mine is a he, I'll stick with the masculine form) is your BFF of the spirit world. He's your best man or maid of honor at your wedding. You chose your communicator guide (and he accepted the challenge) because you have a good relationship, and understand each other well. The problem is, once you're born into this life, it's like a coconut fell on your head, and you can't even remember his name, let alone who he is. It's like you're at the trial all by yourself, and don't even realize you HAVE a co-counsel.

It is possible, however, to re-establish contact and to build a relationship. A good way to do this is through a guided meditation (there's that Moral of the Story One again...), but there are other ways. Once you've met your guide, you can slowly build a relationship. It's just like meeting a new human friend: You start slowly, ask questions, and get to know each other. I'll share my approach in the hope that it will help you.

During a meditation guided by Diana, I met my guide. Of course, I didn't believe any of the information in the meditation, because I thought I was just making stuff up in my head. For one thing, my guide looked suspiciously like Legolas in "The Lord of the Rings." He was beautiful, and had long, silken blond hair. For a girl who had frizzy, short, out-of-control hair and was hopelessly awkward around boys, it seemed highly improbable that I would have this studmuffin of a spirit guide. (Trusting the information I receive has always been my biggest challenge.) Nevertheless, I continued with the process, even though I was skeptical and felt pretty silly most of the time.

Sometimes I would begin a "conversation" with him during meditations and see what answer came to me. Sometimes I would ask a question and begin journaling until the answer revealed itself. Sometimes I would ask for a sign to confirm something, and simply wait for an answer. This was how I found out his name. I call him "Val."

Usually, during meditations I simply ask Val whether he has any messages he can share with me. Eventually, I started to get information that not only was completely counter to what I wanted to hear, but that later proved to be true. This was when I started believing in the process.

For example, when I was searching for a job, I finally landed an interview for one that I thought would be perfect. The interview went so well that I thought I was assured of an offer. During meditation, I thanked Val for his help, and asked if I would get the job. "No," came the answer, "but don't worry. Something better will come along."

No? No??!! I began to throw a bit of a spiritual hissy fit. *Surely I'm misunderstanding. I nailed the interview. The job is perfect. What the hell do you mean "NO"???!!!*

But I didn't get the job. And in retrospect, it would not have been the right position for me. And something better did come along.

Now that I've come to accept the whole idea of spirit guides, here's another way I like to think about it. I often envision life as a movie, and we're the actors. Then I imagine our spiritual support staff watching us as they would a movie, eating popcorn and shouting at the screen. "No! Don't go outside! It's not safe!" Or, "I wouldn't trust him if I were you. Seems like he's hiding something." If we have no relationship with them, we can't hear them, and, like the characters in the movie, simply go about playing our roles.

But what if we do begin to develop a relationship with them? What if we start to become aware that they're watching, and begin to hear what they're shouting at the screen? Imagine you're watching a movie, and you yell, "Don't go in the basement!" And instead of going in, the character cocks her ear, listens, and turns to the camera and says, "So you're telling me it's not safe in the basement?" How cool would that be? It would be more like playing an interactive video game than watching a movie. And, with the benefit of those who can see further than you can.

And all for the low, low price of... nothing.

If you're uncomfortable with the idea of a spirit guide and developing a relationship with an unseen being, then just think of it as getting in touch with your subconscious, or your higher self, or tapping into your intuition. Because whatever you call it or whatever makes sense to you, a wealth of information is available to us and there for the asking.

Chapter 4

The Voices in My Head

*"Before you diagnose yourself as being depressed, or with low self-esteem,
first make sure you're not, in fact, just surrounding yourself with assholes."*

~ William Gibson

"Marry me. Please, please will you marry me?"

I looked into his pleading, dark brown eyes, ran my fingers through his perfect hair, sighed, and snuggled deeper into his strong arms. Oddly, my mind flashed to the movie *The Blues Brothers*, when John Belushi's character, laying in a sewer pipe and covered in mud, comes up with a series of ridiculous excuses as to why he left Carrie Fisher's character waiting at the altar, all the while pleading with his eyes. My Jon had those same eyes, though I was the one coming up with the excuses.

I-I've already been married three times. I-I-I'm only recently divorced. I don't know if I even want to be married again. We've only known each other a short time. It would be crazy. The craziest thing I've ever done. I would have to move to Indiana. I have too many pets. I-I-I-...

"I don't know," was all that came out.

"Please."

"I don't ever want to go through another divorce again." I said. "If we were, you know, to marry, it would have to be the last time. I can't go through that again. I can't."

"I agree."

"What if I can't find a job? The economy is still horrible, you know."

"Who cares? I make more than enough for both of us. Work, don't work, volunteer. I just want you to be happy." That last word trailed off as his eyes became even softer and as pleading as a golden retriever puppy asking for a treat.

Silence. "You're still looking at me," I said, after what seemed like an eternity.

This last year had been a whirlwind. A divorce. An unexpected romance that exploded between two former acquaintances. When Jon shined his light on me, it was almost overwhelming. I had never felt so completely...taken care of. So protected and safe. There was nothing he wouldn't do for me. No luxury too frivolous, no need unmet. Oh, it would be so nice to have that all the time, instead of having to steal time together due to the distance that separated us.

What if this were my last chance at happiness? Wouldn't I regret always wondering more than I would regret failure?

"O.k." I found myself saying.

"O.k.?"

"O.k. Yes."

And so began another whirlwind of planning and preparing. When the day came to turn in my resignation, I hesitated. "Are you sure?" I asked. "Speak now or forever hold your peace."

"The only time I want to hear that," he replied, "is before I say 'I do.' I've never been more sure about anything."

Funny story: After the ceremony, on an idyllic, private beach, a sudden storm unleashed torrential rains just as we reached the safety of our beach house.

"Whew!" we said, laughing as we ducked inside. "Hope that's not a sign!"

Eh…yeah…LOL.

The first time he told me he wanted a divorce was at Thanksgiving, ten months into our marriage. What began as a fairly run-of-the-mill argument ended with Jon dropping the D-bomb.

My response was anything but dignified. I panicked. I cried. I engaged in emotional manipulation designed to keep my very world from falling apart. The next day, overcome by guilt, Jon pleaded with me not to go in the same way he had asked me to marry him.

Dr. Denial lifted one corner of the rug, while Captain Cliché fetched the broom. The pile was neatly swept under, and the corner of the rug allowed to fall back into place. Life went on as if nothing had happened.

It was the same scenario nine months later. And again a year later. Lather, rinse and repeat.

That was when I started noticing the voices. Not literally, mind you – I wasn't having auditory hallucinations. But those nagging thoughts, the ones Dr. Denial had for the most part so effectively managed to keep at bay, were back in earnest. And with my self-esteem in the crapper, no job, a largely otherwise-occupied husband, no friends nearby, and dreary, rainy, rapidly shortening days, those voices pretty much had free rein.

You idiot. What made you think this time would be any better than your other marriages? All the warning signs were there. All of them! Before you ever said yes! There were more red flags waving than at a parade in China. But did you see any of them? Nooooo… Why the hell not? You gave up your life for this. Gave it up! Now you're unemployed. And old. Nobody hires people your age anymore. They all want 20-somethings. How are you even going to survive? Here you've had every opportunity, every need provided, for ten whole months, and you still don't know what you want to do with your new life! No wonder he doesn't want you around. What a screw up.

No. I can make this work. Really. I'll do better. I just need to stop doing those things that annoy him.

Yeah, right. Well, you'd better. Don't mess this up, or you're really screwed.

As I sat and tried in vain to keep the nagging thoughts at bay, I looked around the room. It was 9:00, past Jon's bedtime. The living room was in another part of the house, and if I kept the volume on the t.v. turned way down, it didn't keep him awake. My eyes traveled from the ridiculously big t.v. to the beautiful fireplace with its empty mantle. There was little else to fill the room, except for the furniture. What color was that, anyway? Olive green? I sighed. Whatever it was, it was not one of my favorite colors.

Just say it. It's fugly.

Yeah, o.k., it's hideous.

You got rid of most everything you owned for this? What were you thinking, moving into his home? That he built with his ex-wife? Are you crazy? This will never be your home. Never.

Wrapped in a blanket, I struggled to reach my glass of wine without disturbing my two cats who were draped across me at various angles. The house didn't just look cold – it was cold. Winter, summer, it didn't matter. I was only partially successful in my reach, and one of the cats jumped off, almost causing a spill. Red wine, no less. Talk about a disaster.

You know, you could quit feeling sorry for yourself. You don't like it, then change it. It IS your home too. For better or for fugly.

That's actually a good thought, for a change. It would be fun. We could pick out new furniture together. Have lunch afterwards. Planning, spending money, eating – things we could both agree on.

"No," he said, barely looking up from his reading.

"No?"

"No. I like the furniture."

"Oh. Well, I don't really care for it."

"Well, I like it. And since I like it, it wouldn't be an improvement. It would just be a waste of money." He continued reading.

Not to me it wouldn't.

"Well, o.k. It was just a thought."

Well, that was a stupid idea now, wasn't it? And anyway, he's right. You wear this giant rock of a ring on your finger. You just got a sporty new car. And now you want to spend even more money? He is right. You really are selfish.

"So, leave for dinner in an hour or so?"

"No."

"No?"

"I don't feel like it anymore. I think I'll just go to bed early."

"But I'm showered and almost ready to ..."

"I said I'm going to bed early. I don't want to talk now. I'm exhausted."

"...go. Okay...." I left the room.

I told you...don't bring this up.

No you didn't! You told me TO bring this up!

Now you went and poked the bear. You could at least have waited 'til after dinner.

Yeah, I'll remember that next time I have a stupid idea.

The next morning, Jon called from work. He was silly, charming, joking around.

See? Everything's fine. He still loves me.

"So guess what? Jenna's coming for a visit! Uh-huh, uh-huh, uh-huh…whoo-hoo!" he chanted in a sort of verbal happy dance.

"Oh, wonderful!" I said, hoping the enthusiasm in my voice was masking the dread in my stomach. *Oh, yayyy…*the voice in my head trailed off into high-pitched unenthusiasm.

Jenna, his daughter, was in her third year of college. The light of Jon's life, she had every right to be an entitled, spoiled brat. Except she wasn't. She was smart, lovely and fun, and I was generally in awe of her bubbly personality.

So why was it that every time she visited, Jon and I got into an argument that shook the very foundation of our marriage? I never knew what it would be about, or when it would occur. I never knew whether it would be something I said, something I didn't say, something I did, or some thought that was apparent on my face. I only knew that it was inevitable, and that it would be my fault. I checked the bottle in my allotted bathroom drawer. Thank god. I still had plenty of Xanax.

O.k. Try to get it right this time. Remember, this isn't about you, I reminded myself as I cleaned her room. Fridge stocked? Favorite ice cream in freezer? Movie rented? Comfort food in the oven? Check, check and check.

After her visit, we stood and waved at her as she disappeared down the street. *Buh-bye.* I breathed a huge sigh of relief as I realized that I had made it through her visit without an argument with Jon. *See? Things were getting better!*

"So," I said, placing my arm around him and drawing him close, "that was fun, don't you think?"

"Yeah, right," he said, pulling away and disappearing into the house.

I stared, dumbfounded, before hurrying after him. "Is something wrong?"

"You were awful. What is wrong with you?"

I searched my memory for any clue as the pit in my stomach grew. "Uh, not sure what you mean ..."

"Why did you have to storm out of the room when we were watching the movie?"

Storm out? I replayed the events of the previous evening in my mind. "Sorry, guys. I can't watch this anymore," I said. "The violence is getting to me. You keep watching. I'm going to go into the other room and watch something else." Was that storming out? I didn't think I did. I did leave abruptly, though, after the horse got punched in the head. Somehow the disclaimer that "no animals were harmed while making this movie" never seemed to provide any comfort.

"Oh, you were so angry. I could see it on your face. Why do you always have to make it all about you? You ruined the whole evening."

I continued to stare as he turned and walked away. The all-too-familiar feeling of wanting to disappear into a hole in the ground was overwhelming. That being impossible, I did the next most logical thing: I sat down and just began sobbing. I couldn't seem to stop. The phrase *"ruined the whole evening"* kept replaying in my mind like a broken record.

I ran into the bathroom, barely closing the door in time before really letting loose. The rage enveloped me like a fog on steroids. Together with panic, it welled up from the pit in my stomach to my throat. How DARE he??!! ASSHOLE!!! I grabbed the nearest bottle of lotion and hurled it against the wall. Then a bottle of shampoo. Anything I could get my hands on. Shampoo mixed with lotion flowed down the wall to make a bizarre, new 2-in-1 product. Oh, it felt good! Too good! But it didn't last. I stared at the dents in the wall and the mess in the tub.

As my dog would have said, "Ruh-roh."

That evening, once again alone after he went to bed, I found myself talking to Val, to anyone who might be listening.

"I'm sorry. I can't do this anymore. I just can't. I don't see a way forward. I have nowhere to go, no way to support myself. I don't see a way out of this mess I've created. I'm sorry I've let you all down. Really. But I don't want to go on. I've been given so much, and I've just wasted all of it. And for what? Some guy who I thought was different? He doesn't even want me around. Everything I do is wrong. I can't do it anymore. I just can't. I always screw everything up." Rewind. Repeat.

Sigh. How would I go about it? I looked at the gun that I had taken out of Jon's nightstand, now on the table next to me. No, too scary. I knew I wouldn't be able to pull the trigger. What I really wanted was to just not wake up. Gas? Carbon monoxide? Where? Not in the house. That would completely ruin the house.

See? I'm not entirely selfish, am I?

Pills? Those might work. I didn't know. I was exhausted. Not tonight. Tomorrow. If I could just make it through the night, tomorrow I could end it. Procrastination, as I had come to learn, is an excellent deterrent to suicide.

It's amazing how sometimes the most significant things in our lives begin in a completely unremarkable way. How a seemingly insignificant or off-hand comment by someone, or something I've heard a million times before, suddenly sticks in my mind and is truly understood. So it was with this.

I had made it through the night, and awakened to that initial wonderful moment in which I had not yet recalled the events of the previous day.

Oh, yeah. Jon and I were at it again. Wanting to die. Yup, now I remember. Pills best option. Tomorrow. I'll get to that tomorrow. Right now I just have to make it through the day. Now, how the hell am I going to do that?

I checked my email, and found a reply to a message I had sent some days earlier. I had never actually met the sender in person, but as a friend of a friend, she was a sort of e-kindred spirit. In my message, I had thanked her for some words of encouragement she sent.

"Your timing is impeccable," I wrote. "There's nothing quite so able to fuel the fire of low self-esteem like job hunting."

"Yeah, what's up with that low self-esteem thing?" she wrote in her reply. "Why are we always so mean and saying bad things to ourselves? We need to just stop it."

Just stop it. Just stop it. Just stop saying bad things to ourselves. Stop it.

Just like the phrase "ruined the whole evening," these words now reverberated through my head.

I thought of Eckhart Tolle, whose books had had such an impact on me (at least, what I could grasp of them). He, too, had battled depression much of his life, and had experienced a profound awakening. It started with him uttering the phrase, "I cannot live with myself any longer."

Been there, Eck.

He wrote: "This was the thought that kept repeating itself in my mind. Then suddenly, I became aware of what a peculiar thought it was. 'Am I one or two? If I cannot live with myself, there must be two of me: the 'I' and the 'self' that 'I' cannot live with.' "Maybe," I thought, "only one of them is real."

Stop saying bad things to ourselves. Who is saying these things? And to whom? How can I talk to myself if I am one entity?

But I'm not one entity, am I? Not really. Freud may have gotten a lot of things wrong, but one thing he seems to have gotten right was the part about the ego. And my ego, instead of doing its job and helping me to navigate and make sense out of my daily world, was instead attacking me. My ego had chosen to believe all the bad things that were ever said to me, and was now my own worst enemy.

I suddenly had this vision of my heart, vulnerable and defenseless, surrounded by the rest of me. My soul, my spirit, if you will, was nestled within my heart. My body, my ego, my earthly self, surrounded it. I envisioned myself as two layers – a soft core and a harder candy coating that was my outer layer.

If my outer layer didn't protect my core, my being, who would? Seriously, who would? Jon, who had sworn to honor and protect me? No. In fact, he was the main person from whom I felt I had to protect myself. My family? No.

Sadly, though without meaning it, they were the ones who taught me to be so critical and judgmental. My friends? That's not their job. The only person who can and should protect me, is me. And I was doing a sucky job of it.

In my case, not only was my outer-self failing to protect my inner-self, it was trying to destroy it. The one friend I'm supposed to have is not only spineless, but has joined forces with the enemy. So my core, my heart, my soul – whatever I wanted to call it – has two choices: put up walls and defenses, or surrender. Give up. Die. I was no longer able to maintain my walls. Jon's precision arrows, knowingly or not, were perfectly aimed at my most vulnerable spots, causing the walls to crumble at their very foundations.

My core deserved at least one friend, at least one person on its side, and that person had to be me. Maybe I would not be enough. Maybe I wasn't very strong right now. But at the very least I had to stop making things worse.

I had to stop saying bad things to myself.

And I did. Then and there. Like the lifelong smoker who snuffs out her last cigarette and never touches them again, I vowed I would stop. I would be my own protector and best friend.

That's not to say I didn't have slips. In the beginning, I had to actively counteract the voice until my brain got the hang of it. Like the smoker, I would have cravings, enjoy inhaling secondhand smoke, or look longingly at the brightly colored packs encased in glass behind the check-out counter. So, for a while, my conversations would go something like this:

You idiot.

You're not an idiot. You're actually a very smart person.

What made you think this time would be any better than your other marriages? All the warning signs were there. All of them!

You love Jon. You trusted him and believed what he told you. That doesn't make you stupid. It makes you human.

You gave up your entire life for this. Gave it up!

Well, you made the most logical choice you could at the time. And remember what I just told you: You trusted, loved and believed. What kind of a person would you be if you couldn't do that?

Who would even hire you? You're too old.

That's bullshit. You're healthy, active and really good at what you do. You will find the right company. And they'll be lucky to have you.

How are you even going to survive? Here you've had every opportunity, every need provided, for ten whole months, and you still don't know what you want to do with your new life? No wonder he doesn't want you around. What a screw-up.

Ten whole months, huh? That's not long to rebuild an entire life under the best of circumstances, let alone on constantly shifting sands. You gave up your job, your home, your friends and even your name, and have to live with your very foundation, your security, constantly being threatened. That's a lot to handle for anyone. So you don't have all the answers. Yet. That doesn't make you a screw-up. Far from it. So just stop it. You're done.

Sometimes I'm not sure I believed my own arguments against my inner voice. But good attorneys are able to argue both sides of an issue, even if it goes against their personal beliefs, and so I fought back anyway. Eventually, I must have gotten tired of arguing with myself. Or maybe my heart, my core, finally started to believe that someone had its back. Whatever the reason, the horrible internal dialogues came to an end.

I'd only heard this a million times. "We are our own worst enemy." "Words can hurt." "Thoughts are powerful." And my favorite: "No one can make you feel inferior without your consent." There was no shortage of ammunition for Captain Cliché. Like so many things, I agreed with this, I knew it, but I didn't get it. Now I got it. I would never let myself speak to me that way again.

I didn't know it at the time, but the day I vowed to "just stop it" was the last day I would suffer from depression. It was the last time I would not want to live. It was the beginning of being able to look in the mirror and genuinely love what I saw. After a lifetime of wondering when the next time would be that I would be standing at the edge of the proverbial cliff wanting to step off, I could now, at last, simply enjoy the view.

MORAL OF THE STORY FOUR:
STOP SAYING MEAN THINGS TO YOURSELF

Stop negative self-talk. Seriously. Just cut it out.

Like meditation, this takes commitment, awareness and practice. Like meditation, when you catch your thoughts going somewhere you don't want them to, just gently and calmly bring them back to where you would like them to be. Don't be harsh. Don't be judgmental. Be as patient and as calm as you would be with a young child. And be as firm as you would be with that child to stop him from running in front of a car. It's simply not acceptable.

If it's helpful, envision yourself as having two layers. Envision your heart (your inner core) surrounded by an outer layer (your human self, your ego – however you want to imagine or name it). Now think of these as two members of the same football team.

Your inner core is the quarterback, and your outer layer is his best offensive lineman. This guy plows head first into the thick of things and does all he can to protect his quarterback, so that the quarterback, in turn, is free to run the play and throw the ball (and with that, you now pretty much have the extent of my understanding of football).

Now imagine what would happen if the lineman not only didn't do his job, but turned around and began to tackle the quarterback? Imagine how hard it would be for the quarterback to even get a pass thrown when he has to be fending off his own teammate. Eventually he would be flat on the ground, injured, or worse. This is what it's like when you are your own worst enemy.

Your heart's job, your core being's job, is to just be. To be you, to feel joy, to be happy, to give love, to receive love, to feel compassion. I believe it houses the spark of our creator that we are born with. Your outer layer, your ego, is there to interface and interact with the world. Its job is also to protect your core, not to turn on it. Don't let it.

Just stop it.

Chapter 5

15 Hands, 15 Years Old

Horses are God's apology for men.

~ Unknown

During this time of darkness, literally and figuratively, the few bright spots were my visits to the stables. My inexplicable love of all things horses, in remission since childhood, had been rekindled on the high mesas of New Mexico. Despite having willingly sacrificed my possessions, self-esteem and power on the altar of marriage, somehow this rekindled flame had survived the move to Indiana.

Those who nurture the horse-flame in their hearts understand the impact of simply walking into a barn. The calm, the otherworldliness, the smell. Oh, the smell! That indescribable, trade-secret-of-God mix of... what? Wood shavings, dirt, horse poop, horse sweat, and some other ingredient known only to Him. He then blessed the flame-nurturers with a patented special sensor that allows them to smell it, which in turn, triggers the release of endorphins and simultaneously registers the smell of horse poop as inoffensive. Because as any flame-nurturer will attest, horse poop does not stink.

By many twists of fate that seem miraculous in hindsight, I had found a barn where I was able to ride one or two days a week. The horse's owner was away at college, and I think both he and I were grateful for the diversion. But as I watched the other women building relationships with their own horses, I began to wonder what that would be like. To not have to ask permission. To not have to worry that I would do something to confuse, or worse somehow harm, another person's beloved horse. To not have to remind myself not to become too attached, because one day he might be moved to be with his owner. Or worse, be sold.

And so it was one day that I told the barn owner that if her emails included the offer of a horse for sale that would be a good match for me, I would be open to it.

"What kind of horse are you looking for?" she asked.

"Uh, I dunno," I replied.

"Mare or gelding?"

"Yes," I said, laughing. "Definitely a mare or a gelding."

"O.k. You gotta give me something to go on other than four hooves, a mane and a tail."

Fair enough.

"I want a horse who is about 15 years old and about 15 hands tall. Old enough to know what he's doing, big enough that I won't feel guilty asking him to carry me, and not so big that I wouldn't be able to mount from the ground. But I'm not in a hurry. If it takes a year, that's fine."

"That's it?" she asked with raised eyebrows.

"Well, it'd be nice if he likes me too."

Two weeks later, I was heading out to see a horse named Jefe. I knew that word from my time in New Mexico. Pronounced "Heh-fay," it means "Boss."

"I know this horse," the barn owner had told me. "And his owner. He brought him out here for a clinic once. I would have bought him on the spot if he were for sale. You'll have some issues to overcome, but nothing we can't handle."

I didn't ask what color he was, or how much he was asking. Just the phone number.

Oy, I'm so nervous! What do I ask? How do I not come across as someone who has never bought a horse before, when I've never bought a horse before? What if he isn't right for me, but I'm too embarrassed to say, and then I wind up buying him anyway because he looks at me with big brown eyes? Oh, my Achilles heel… big, soft, brown eyes. So unless he has blue eyes, I'm screwed. Oh, this was the worst idea ever. What am I doing? You know, I'll just keep borrowing horses. Maybe lease one. Yeah, that's it. Leasing will be fine.

As I entered the barn, there was no magical horse smell. Instead, the faint smell of urine permeated the air. Then I saw him. A strong, broad back with beautiful brown and white markings and a touch of black in his mane and tail.

Just like the pictures of horses I used to draw when I was a little girl. Brown and white with a black mane and tail. That way they had a little bit of every color and I didn't have to choose.

I watched him roll in his small paddock. "Yup, he likes to roll, all right," said his owner. "So you never have to groom him. He's self-grooming, that one."

I laughed, trying to choose between several witty replies that had popped into my head all at once. *Does he blanket himself too when it gets too cold out? Can he clean his own tack? How about shoes – do I need to call the farrier, or is he a self-shoer?* Then I realized the owner was serious.

And to think I was the one afraid of looking like an idiot.

"How old is he?" I asked.

"Sixteen."

Off by a year, but close enough.

"Oh, wait," he said, looking at his registration papers. "Nope, I did the math wrong. He's fifteen." I took the papers from him and checked the math. Foaled two days after my birthday. A fellow Taurus.

"Do you know how tall he is?" I asked.

"About 15 hands."

And so it was that I broke the first rule of horse shopping, and bought the first horse I looked at. I also informed Jon of the cardinal rules of horse ownership:

1. There will always be something I need to buy.
2. I will never be home when I say I will be.

I felt as giddy as a schoolgirl who finds out that the boy she's had a crush on for like, ever, happens to, you know, like her back. The first thing I fell in love with was his long mane, tangled and matted despite his valiant efforts at self-grooming. Next it was his pink, wrinkled muzzle that made him look like an old man.

Jefe was a kind horse, though as I came to know him and more about his past, I believe he would have been justified in becoming mean and bitter. Instead, he had learned to shut down. I suppose that to many people, he would have just seemed obedient. But to me, the unblinking eyes told me that his mind was somewhere else. "Do with me what you will," he seemed to be saying, "but just get it over with as quickly and as painlessly as possible."

I decided that this sensitive horse with the old soul and matted mane needed a new beginning. And so I called him Phoenix, after the beautiful bird that rises from the ashes and whose tears are said to be healing. Looking back, I wonder whether he rose from his own ashes, or from mine.

As I untangled his mane, he began to untangle the loneliness and self-doubt I still carried after moving back to Indiana. I had the shoes removed that were restricting his feet, and he began to remove the hurt restricting my heart. And as I worked hard to gain his trust, he showed me that it has to go both ways. It's not enough for him to trust me. I have to trust him too. And trust myself. That was a whole lot of something that had never come easily to me.

He started teaching me this the first time I saw him run loose in the arena. I stood in the middle, watching him run, stick and attached string in hand, well aware that he could at any time turn and run toward me. Or even kick out at me. But he didn't. He trotted his beautiful, floating trot, broke into a canter, stopped suddenly, tossed his head, spun gracefully and changed direction as if he were cutting some invisible calf from a herd.

"Oh, wow," I whispered, breathless.

And then he stopped a short distance away, turning to face me. Again he tossed his head, blowing a giant snort, looking at me expectantly.

"What did you think of that?" he seemed to ask.

"Oh, Phoenix...that was beautiful. You are amazing!"

He lowered his head, and stood quietly, licking his lips. "May I?"

"Yes."

And with that, he approached slowly, hesitantly. I reached out and stroked his shoulder as he stood near me, blowing, breathing, being.

This was love. Horse love. I even had documented proof. It came in the form of an online quiz. I could never resist a good quiz.

According to psychologist Robert Sternberg, the three components of love are intimacy, passion and commitment. Three legs of a triangle, all three necessary for a strong, stable love. With a simple quiz, I could assess these three legs of my intimate relationship. The instructions were to rate each statement on a scale of 1 to 9, filling in each blank with the name of my significant other. Honestly, it looked like something from a magazine I would read while having my hair done, but it was on the internet and mentioned a well-known researcher, so it had to be valid, right?

Question: I would rather be with _____ than with anyone else. Would I rather be with Jon than anyone else? That depends (said the lawyer), on which Jon happened to show up. If Jon v.1, then absolutely. But Jon v.2, who put in his first appearance shortly after our wedding? In that case, I'd rather be with just about anyone else, though I might just as well be alone.

Yeah, well, you're pretty good at closing yourself off too.

That's enough, you. Remember our deal about no more talking smack. Even if you do have a point.

Phoenix, however, had only one version. So, actually, I believe I would rather be with Phoenix than with anyone else. Maybe I'm doing this all wrong and filling in the wrong name. Let's try again.

Question: Just seeing Phoenix excites me. Well, yes, seeing Phoenix does excite me. That little display in the arena? Nothing is more exciting or more beautiful to me than that.

Question: I find myself thinking about Phoenix during the day. Constantly. And when I do, I have to smile inside like the cat who just ate the canary. He also provides the perfect antidote to spousal irritations.

Jon: "Sweetie, I'll be playing poker tonight with the boys."

Me: "Sounds good." *Stay out the whole stupid night for all I care. I'll be with my horse.*

Jon: "Sweetie, I want to buy [insert name of some expensive thing] for Jenna [that she doesn't need].

Me: "Have fun shopping. " *Remember Rule #1! And he deserves the best too!*

Jon: "Sweetie, I'm going to spend half the weekend watching [insert sport] on t.v."

Me: "Enjoy!" *Whatever. I'll be spending half my weekend with my horse.*

Question: I find Phoenix to be personally very attractive. Oh, yes! Every time I look at him, I think how handsome he is. How strong, how beautifully spotted, how his long mane flows like Fabio's. He's definitely attractive.

Question: I cannot imagine another person making me as happy as Phoenix does. Oh, that's a no-brainer. Have I been happier with Jon? Absolutely. But Phoenix ALWAYS makes me happy. I can be having the crappiest day, or be in the depths of despair, and he makes me happy. He never criticizes, never points out things I've done wrong, and all of his jokes are funny. He even likes my singing. I think.

Question: I especially like physical contact with Phoenix. Oh, definitely! I especially love riding him bareback, feeling every muscle, feeling stable and safe. I love brushing his mane, kissing his nose, rubbing his tired neck and back muscles after a ride. Oh, I definitely love physical contact with Phoenix.

And finally: There is something "magical" about my relationship with Phoenix. Oh yes. One day, as he stood in his stall and I stood on the other side of the door, he looked at me. He looked right in my eye, and held the gaze. That moment was indescribable. There was a knowing, a connection, however brief, in which so much was said without a spoken word. THAT was magical.

When I added up the scores, it was clear: I was in love with my horse. Head-over-heels. After all, internet test scores don't lie. I guess that makes me strange, but my guess is that there are a lot of other weirdoes like me out there. And most of us are women.

Apology accepted. Thanks, God.

MORAL OF THE STORY FIVE:
ASK FOR WHAT YOU WANT

Remember that personal support staff in the spirit world we talked about? The other members of your legal team? Turns out, they – along with the guardian angels that many of us learned about from a young age - really want to help us. They love nothing more than to be of assistance. But here's the catch: They can't do so unless we ask. Under the rules, our helpers cannot simply unilaterally decide one day to grant wishes we never made.

Actually, my understanding is that there are a number of rules surrounding the granting of requests which, if written in the form of a legal contract, I imagine might look something like this:

1. Higher Beings (hereinafter, "Grantors") shall be available at all times to receive Requests of any nature from an Earthly Being (hereinafter, "Requestor"), whether made orally, in writing, or by any other means.

2. Said Request shall be granted, unless:
    i. The Request restricts the Free Will of another Being.
    ii. The Request is likely to result in undue harm to the Requestor.
    iii. The Request is in contradiction to the terms of the Agreement entered into between Requestor and Requestor's Support Staff prior to incarnation in the earth plane, otherwise known as "birth."

3. No Grants shall originate from a Grantor. As it is understood that Earthly Beings are in possession of Free Will, Grantors are expressly

prohibited from initiating action in support of a Requestor without receipt of an appropriate Request, as outlined in (1). This prohibition may not be overridden by good intentions of the Grantor.

4. Whereas receiving and granting Requests is mandatory, subject to the provisions outlined in Section 2 subsections i. – iii., no limitations are placed upon Grantors as to the manner or timeframe in which the Request is to be granted.

Translation:
1. All prayers will be heard.
2. Ask and you shall receive.
3. You have to ask in order to receive.
4. Exactly how and when your prayers/intentions are answered might be different than you had envisioned, so be careful what you ask for.

In regard to point 4, I personally believe that it's best to err on the side of vagueness in your requests. In other words, ask for the final result you want, and leave how it happens to those who are helping you. For example, when I was looking for a horse, my stated intention – my request – was simply "to find the perfect horse for me, preferably about 15 years old and about 15 hands tall." Could I have asked for a brown and white gelding with a beautiful black and white mane? Sure. But what if the perfect horse for me wasn't a paint, or was a mare, or 16 hands tall? In the end, don't we just want the right one?

Therefore, a common intention or prayer that I use is to simply ask for the "highest good for all concerned." For example, if I have a friend who is dealing with relationship issues, I would ask that "the situation be resolved with the highest good and with blessings and comfort for all concerned." Could I ask that the couple resolve their issues? Or that my friend finally see the light and dump the rat bastard? Sure. But I don't know what's best, do I? All I can ask is that it be resolved as painlessly as possible.

The point is, intentions are powerful. You can pray, write in a journal, ask during a meditation, or simply have a conversation with your guide while out walking your dog. It can't hurt, right? Heck, even my dogs figured that out. Never mind I just gave them a treat 5 minutes ago - it never hurts to ask for another one.

So just try it. You might be really pleasantly surprised.

Chapter 6

It Seemed Like a Good Idea at the Time

"I'm not crazy, I've just been in a very bad mood for 40 years!"

~ From the movie
"Steel Magnolias"

Oh, this was a bad idea. I shouldn't have come. I think I'll leave. There's no receptionist. No one around. I can just sneak out quietly, and it'll be like I never showed up. Now or never, though, before she comes to get me. Abort mission! Abort mission! Crap. Here she comes. Too late. Say nothing, act casual.

My eyes quickly scanned the small office as I sat down. It was cozy - a typical female counselor's office. There were artsy metal wall hangings, and framed abstract works that were open to interpretation. A fountain, tucked in the corner, bubbled discretely.

"So what brings you in today?"

Well, nothing too serious. I'm just batcrap crazy is all, and I'm kind of at wits end, and I read about this treatment method in in one of my counseling courses, and since it was developed by a real live woman and not by some old dead white guy, I thought maybe, just maybe, it might be better than all the other questionable-at-best approaches out there, so I did some searching and found you.

Yeah. O.k. Maybe filter that a bit.

"I'm taking some courses in clinical counseling, and read about EMDR in one of my textbooks. Honestly, the case study hit home and it caught my attention. All I know is, sometimes someone says or does some little thing that hits me the wrong way, and I go from being a fairly reasonable adult to acting like a 3-year old child."

"O.k. That's understandable," Ruth said, nodding. "Tell me what you know about EMDR."

"Well, I know it stands for Eye Movement Desensitization and Reprocessing, and that it's used to help people who suffer from PTSD. I don't completely understand how it works, but I know it involves inducing eye movements from side to side, and at the same time, recalling memories. My understanding is, it helps the brain process traumatic events that, at the time, sent us into overload."

"Well, you already understand more than most people who come to see me, so congratulations. And to be honest, we're still not completely sure how it works, although we do have our theories. I kind of like to envision it as using a plunger on the brain. You know how a toilet or sink can get stopped up, and then all it takes is one good plunge, and all of a sudden things start to flow again? Kind of like that."

I couldn't help but laugh out loud, enjoying the vision of a plunger stuck to the top of my head.

That'll be $200 please. And the plunger is yours to keep.

"What I'm not sure about, is that when I read about the reactions of the trauma survivors in the case studies, it really rang true with so much of my experiences. But..." I hesitated, not sure how to continue. Ruth simply continued to look at me, patiently.

"... I've never suffered any trauma. Not that I'm aware of, at least. I've never been shot at, or in a war zone, or beaten, or raped, or in a serious accident. And to be honest, I'm not sure I believe half the cases I hear about in which people "suddenly" remember horrible childhood abuse. Not that it can't happen. I just think it's sometimes a little too…convenient."

"I would agree. And I do think it's possible to induce false memories. However, that's not possible with EMDR. Or it shouldn't be. Because the prompts are very simple. They really don't suggest anything to you, but simply guide you to the next step. You do all the work. And you can do as much or as little of that out loud as you want. You don't have to share anything if you don't want to."

She paused to let this sink in before continuing. "But back up a bit. How about you tell me something about the latest incident in which you suddenly started feeling and acting like a 3-year old?"

"Well, like many things I suppose, it seemed like a good idea at the time."

The text was so long it was broken into four separate messages, but the gist was this: A horse buddy had a cabin in Michigan. There was a rental cabin nearby that would sleep four, and had stalls for horses. Easy access to lots of trails. Anyone interested in a girls trip? We could all trailer our horses up together for a week of trail riding and relaxation.

A girl's trip?! A week of trail riding?! No way!! It just didn't get any better. Three others had already decided to go when I wrote "I'm in!" before hitting send.

My excitement was mixed with a little anxiety, though. I had just bought my first trailer, and only had a couple of short hauls under my belt. A four hour drive on busy interstates would be a different story. Just the thought of pulling into a gas station with that thing behind me was scary. And then there was the issue of, well, me. I wasn't always good in groups of people, especially those whom I didn't know too well. And then there was Jon. Things finally, finally seemed to be getting on track between us. Was this the best time to be leaving?

The others reassured me about the trailering. "You'll be fine. We'll be travelling in a group, so if anything goes wrong, you'll have back-up."

Jon's reaction was positive as well. "Go for it. And if you're going to do that, I think I'll take a vacation with Jenna later this summer. You know, father-daughter thing. Maybe go to Oregon, see the redwoods."

Awwww! I've always wanted to do that again. Can't we all go together? No, no...I know...selfish.

And anyway, Jon had made it very clear that where Jenna was concerned, he would do what he wanted, when he wanted, no explanation or permission necessary. This apparently was still a sensitive subject. Sensitive enough that he had stopped sharing details of their many visits with me.

Besides, you've seen the redwoods. And you'll be trail riding. With your own horse. Not even the redwoods could match that. Deal.

The date of departure approached amid a never-ending stream of text messages and Facebook posts. "I'm so excited I could pee my pants!" one of the posts read, followed by a string of emojis.

I was excited, but my pants were in no danger of getting wet. *Must be nerves. About the drive. You'll be fine.*

And I was, once I got Phoenix loaded. We struggled a bit, but once he was in, he quieted down. The drive was more like 5 1/2 hours instead of 4. And the cabin, well, it was beautiful, but although it could technically sleep four, the underlying assumption was that those four people were part of two couples. There were two bedrooms with two full-sized beds. Stacy and her best friend Trisha took one room. That left Sheila and me looking at each other.

"We can share the bed. But I snore like a sailor," she said.

Oh, no. Hell to the no. Which left me on the fold-out sofa bed in the living room. *Ugh. Ok. Ok. No worries. It'll be fine. We're here safe and sound. That's what's most important.*

"Sounds like a typical trip," Ruth said, bringing me back to the present. "There are always unexpected surprises. But why do I sense that there's more 'buts' coming?"

I glanced at my watch to see how much time I had. "How about 'but there I was, with women who all missed their husbands terribly even though they'd all been married for over twenty years?' How about adding to that 'but I wasn't really sure I even missed mine?' How about 'but I was feeling left out of most of the decision-making?' And 'but I couldn't figure out that that any of this was bothering the crap out of me and just thought it was me being grumpy for no reason?'"

"Yeah, that's some big 'buts,'" Ruth said.

"But that's only the beginning. Pun intended," I said, rolling my eyes. I wish I smoked. Just recalling all this made me want to go huddle outside in a doorway all by myself and have something to keep me busy while I did.

"How about you tell me what caused you to start acting like a 3-year old?"

I sighed, struggling once again with what to leave in, what to leave out. "It was my fault, really. All I know is that things started to get chilly. Icy, I mean. Like I said, I was feeling grumpy and left out. I said things that I later found out came across pretty harsh. Then I thought during one of our rides that the others were rude to me. They would whisper to each other and then giggle. I tried to tell myself I was just imagining it."

"Were you?" Ruth asked.

"I don't know. I can be overly sensitive at times. But that started the pit in my stomach. The next day, I said something to the others as were getting ready to go on a ride, and they walked right past me. That was it. My heart sank into my stomach along with the pit that was already there, and I just wanted to leave. I realized this had all been a horrible mistake, and I just wanted to get out of there. To literally disappear."

"So what did you do?"

"We talked that evening. Or tried to. I got defensive. Emotional. Still, I might have been able to handle things, until someone said, 'I never get to go on vacation, and I came here expecting to finally get some relaxation. And instead, I get THIS. You ruined the whole week.' That was it. I broke down. I couldn't stop sobbing. I was crying and inconsolable and throwing a fit like a 3-year old."

"And then what?"

"We talked for a while longer, and they went to bed. I was still upset, though. Feeling a bit panicked. My mind was racing. I didn't sleep the whole night. It made for an interesting drive home the next day."

"Why do you think that upset you so much?"

"Because apparently I have a knack for ruining things, despite making my best efforts. I seem to do that a lot. What is *wrong* with me? I just can't seem to get along with people."

Ruth paused, looking at me intently. "I don't think there's anything wrong with you. But maybe there is something that's stuck. Want to find out?"

"I would love to."

"Put these headphones on. You can close your eyes. You're going to hear a sound – like a clock ticking – that alternates from one ear to the other. I'm going to guide you through the process. You can share as much or as little as you want. You just let me know when you're ready to continue to the next step."

When I had the headphones in place and had adjusted the volume, I looked at Ruth and nodded.

"I want you to go back to the incident you described. What are some of the feelings that come up when you think about this?"

"Tension. Shame. I feel stupid. I ruin everything by just being there. I want to disappear."

"O.k. Good. Do you feel anything in a particular area of your body?"

"I feel that pit in my stomach."

"O.k. If you had to rank these feelings on a scale of 1 – 10, with 1 being bearable and 10 being completely unbearable, how unpleasant would you say you feel when you think about this?"

Oh, if there's anything I hate, it's trying to rank things on a scale of 1 – 10. O.k., fine, just say the first number that pops into your head. "7."

"Good. Now I want you let this go, and think about whether there was another time when you felt this way. Try to just focus on the feeling and let your mind take you wherever it wants to. Don't judge, and don't try to force anything. Take your time."

So I have to think to myself not to think…o.k. If I can meditate, I can do this.

After several minutes had passed, Ruth asked, "Where are you now?"

"I'm with my mother."

"How old are you?"

"Hmm…I'm about 10?"

"O.k. Want to tell me what's going on?"

"My mother is upset with me about something. Something I did, but I can't remember what. She hasn't spoken to me all day, which wasn't unusual. My brother arrives to pick me up. He's invited me to stay with him and his wife for the weekend. She says it's up to me whether to go or not, but I can tell she doesn't really want me to. I decide to go anyway. I try to kiss her on the cheek to say goodbye, but she turns away. I say goodbye and leave."

"What would you say to that 10-year old girl if you could?"

"I'd say that's pretty harsh. That I can't imagine whatever you did was so bad that you deserved to be treated like that. And good for you for trying to do the right thing, saying goodbye instead of just leaving."

"What do your mother's actions say about you?"

"That I must have behaved badly."

Ruth looked at me for what felt like an eternity before finally asking, "Want to try again?"

"What?" I stared at Ruth. I had no idea what to say.

"What do your mother's actions say about you?" she repeated slowly.

I stared down at the floor. *Tick tock tick tock tick tock, one ear other ear one ear other ear.* Finally, I looked up.

"Nothing?"

"That's right. Nothing. HER actions say NOTHING about you. Those are her choices."

She paused to let that sink in. "Do you get that? She reacted that way because of her perception, her stuff. For another person, whatever you did or didn't do might not be

72

a problem at all. Our reactions only say something about us, and our filter through which we view the world."

I heard her, but knew this would take time to sink in. I simply nodded.

"Now I want you to stay with that feeling, and think back to whether there were any other times you felt the same way."

I sat quietly and tried to let my mind wander.

I'm watching my mother lock the doors to the house. She then takes my jump rope, and ties it to the handles of the two doors that face inward at a 90 degree angle to each other. "I'm going upstairs to get some sleep," she says. "If your dad comes home and tries to get in, don't let him."

"Why not?"

"Just don't. It'll ruin everything."

Next thing I remember, my dad is banging at the door. He's really angry. I'm afraid he'll see me through the window if I run upstairs to where my mother is, so I crouch down just inside the door. He continues banging, shouting "Let me in!" Now I'm afraid he'll be able to see me if he gets close to the door and looks down. If he does, there's no telling what he'd do. I make myself into an even smaller ball. He bangs for several minutes before finally leaving. I run upstairs and wake my mother.

"Dad just tried to get in!" I said breathlessly.

"Oh, o.k.," she said before rolling onto her side and going back to sleep.

I fell silent, lost in the feeling of the memory.

"Where are you?" The gentle sound of Ruth's voice breaks through my memory. I tell her what I remembered.

"How old were you?"

"I think about 6 or 7."

"What happened after that?"

"When my mom went back to sleep, I guess I thought it wasn't too important. That it was no big deal. That I was silly for even waking her up. I just left and went back downstairs."

"Alone?"

"Yeah. I was usually alone during the day while she slept. She worked nights."

"Did the two of you talk anymore about it?"

"No. I've never told anyone. I hadn't really thought about this anymore. It's – it's not like I forgot, or repressed it. Like I said, I thought it was no big deal."

"What would you say to that little girl?"

"I'd give her a big hug. I would tell her that it must have been terrifying, and she was very brave. That no one deserves to ever be put in a situation like that, let alone a little kid."

"Exactly. Good job. If you allow your mind to go wherever it wants again, are there any other times you felt the same way?"

I sat quietly, but nothing came up. "No."

"O.k. Now I want you to think back to your trip. To what you described to me. If you had to rank how upsetting this is to you now, how does it feel?"

Ugh, the number thing again. But it was clearly less, and the pit in my stomach was gone.

"About a 3."

Ruth nodded as she made note of this. "Normally we would continue, but this is a pretty powerful memory that's been brought up, so I think we should stop for now. How are you feeling?"

"O.k. Tired."

"Just be gentle with yourself tonight. Go to bed early. And call me if you need to."

I went home to an empty house. Empty, at least, of humans. After dinner, I settled in on the couch and flipped on the t.v. My dog looked at me expectantly, asking to join me. *Just be gentle with yourself tonight.* I patted the seat next to me, and put my arm around her as she curled up at my side.

I thought about the session with Ruth. How could something so seemingly insignificant, so long ago, continue to affect me so much? To reduce me to emotional rubble? Could processing that really have a healing effect? I didn't feel much different. I certainly didn't feel like I'd been plunged.

I had definitely felt different after the Trip from Hell, though. I took the mantra we had adopted of "what happens in Michigan stays in Michigan" literally. Clearly, I had missed some memos about basic human interactions. I didn't want to risk ruining anything else.

The bigger problem was with Phoenix. Now my horse didn't like me either.

After a difficult loading and a 5 ½ hour ride home, he emerged from the trailer with a snort, prancing like an Arabian. We went straight to his pasture, where he jerked away as soon as I unhooked his halter, trotted ten steps, rolled, stood up, and then rolled some more before shaking himself like a dog. The last image I had before leaving was of his large hindquarters trotting off as fast and as far away from me as he could, without looking back. Just as he had done to his previous owner.

"Forget you," he seemed to be saying. "You're just like all the others."

In the days that followed, he actively avoided me when I went to his pasture. Eventually, resigned to the fact that I wasn't leaving, he would let me catch him and slowly lead him inside, but with the same far-away look that I had seen when I first met him. He acted up with the farrier. If he came within sight of the trailer, he would freeze. If I asked him to go closer than 100 feet, he would balk and protest and try his hardest to be anywhere else. He wanted nothing more to do with me or with that rolling, claustrophobic death trap.

Apparently I had ruined things for him too. I wasn't just losing my friends. This was worse. Far worse. I was losing my love.

MORAL OF THE STORY SIX: HEAL TRAUMA

If there's one thing I can't stand, it's the oh-poor-me-I-had-a-crappy-childhood bandwagon. Cry me a river and join the club. None of us survive childhood without TCM's (Traumatic Childhood Memories). That's the definition of childhood, so get over it, and stop making everyone else in your life pay for things they had nothing to do with.

But... what's the difference between using past experiences as an excuse, and acknowledging their effect? Where's the line between wallowing in pain and effectively dealing with it? When is it better to dig up past hurts or to simply accept them and move on? Everyone has buttons that get pushed, right?

In my opinion, when those pushed buttons result in a disproportionate reaction, or begin to disrupt your life and your relationships, you need to consider the possibility of unresolved trauma. And by trauma, I don't mean only shootings, natural disasters or being in a war zone. In fact, I've learned what is traumatic can fall within a surprisingly wide range of experiences. I now understand that it's not so much the experience itself, but its relationship to our ability to process it. This depends on our age, the circumstances – on so many things that, well, all you can say is that "it depends."

In addition to the plunger analogy, I sometimes think of our brains as a landscape, like a field, a hill, or a flood-plain. Rainfall is washed away via ditches, channels, or other well-worn paths – so far so good. Now imagine that so much rain falls at once that the normal drainage paths get backed up. The water has to go somewhere, and as it does, other paths are formed – big paths, formed by a huge amount of fast-moving water. Now the next time rain falls, instead of flowing out through the normal channels, it's much easier and quicker to go through the new, large paths.

When something happens that overwhelms our ability to cope, it's like a deluge of rainfall hitting our brain all at once. The normal processing pathways can't handle the flow, and it has to find other pathways. The problem is that once these pathways are formed, they are very easy for the brain to access again. And so, when something happens that resembles in some way the overwhelming experience, it only makes sense for the brain to allow it to take the easily accessible shortcut. This, in turn, triggers many of the same responses as when it was formed. So if that shortcut was formed as a small child, our reaction will be similar to how that small child would handle things.

Again, this is just my simplistic visualization, but I think this is how our reactions to seemingly "normal" events get blown way out of proportion. Fortunately, many new methods of reprocessing these memories – of plunging or re-landscaping, if you will – are continually being developed. However, I am a fan of EMDR, for reasons that will become clear if you continue reading.

There is another method that I also highly recommend – and this one doesn't require the assistance of a licensed therapist. The book "The Emotion Code," by Dr. Bradley Nelson, was invaluable in my healing process. It's one of my secret weapons in the struggle to become a happier, healthier person.

The premise is that energy, in the form of emotions, can become trapped in our body, wreak havoc on how we feel and react, and can cause physical symptoms and illness, including debilitating pain and even cancer. Most of the time, we aren't even aware that these trapped emotions are there, because they are well-hidden by our subconscious. The Emotion Code process teaches how to use muscle testing to identify and release trapped emotions. It's simple, and can be learned by anyone.

In my case, I had about a gazillion trapped emotions. I had become aware of, and could literally feel, the tension in my chest, around my heart, and in my shoulders that I had carried with me for much of my life. Not only was I able to release the emotions that were blocking my heart, but I also experienced improvement of long-standing allergies, congestion, and a dry cough that has plagued me for over twenty years.

As in other Morals of the Story, however, I ask you to rely on your own research, intuition and comfort level in finding a method that works for you. I only hope you do not, as I did for far too long, simply continue to tell yourself that you need to grow up, tough it out, just accept that you're "a little crazy," or any of the other things the voices in our head tell us. Because dealing with a stopped up drain in your brain means that what should be a walk in the park becomes a slog with hip waders: Possible, but exhausting.

Chapter 7

About Those Lights at the Ends of Tunnels

"You can't argue with crazy."

~ Mom

"The problem is, I have no vision."

"No vision?"

"No imagination," I explained. "I can't look at a single tile and imagine what the entire patio will look like. It just doesn't work that way. I need to see a picture or a drawing."

"How about we think about it. Can you envision a pizza?" Jon asked hopefully.

"Envision, taste, smell, feel the burn on the roof of my mouth...oh, yeah!" And with that, we left the garden center hand in hand, laughing and making Homer Simpson-like drooling noises at the thought of a hot, freshly baked, dripping-with-cheese pizza.

Jon was back. My Jon. Thank god. My horse may hate me, but this partner at least, was back. Sensing my despair and frustration, and probably relieved at not feeling like he was the cause for a change, Jon v. 1.0 - the kind and caring Jon – stepped up.

We finally talked. Really talked. About my uncertainty about what to do with my life. About not being able to find the right job. About my decision to continue with counseling courses. About the law practice I was building. Were these realistic options? Would the risks pay off? Did I have what it takes to do any of these? I was certainly happier than I had been since the move. Our arguments were becoming less frequent. We were even planning some changes to the house, including remodeling the patio and adding a screened-in room, complete with a fountain and meditation bench. Oh, it would be so beautiful! That part, at least, I could envision.

For the first time in our new life together, I was seeing a light at the end of the tunnel.

Phoenix, on the other hand, still wanted nothing to do with the trailer and was less-than-thrilled with me. The way I saw it, I had a few options. I could admit defeat, and find him a new owner. One who was more experienced than I, and who hadn't completely destroyed his trust.

Or I could send him to a trainer to be "fixed." That would be the quicker, though more expensive, solution.

Or I could work with my instructor to solve the problem myself. She would know what to do. Or would she? My trust in other horse people was not very high right now. It seemed like my assumption that all other horse people knew more than me was part of what had gotten me into this situation.

No matter which option I chose, I could probably kiss trail riding goodbye for the rest of the season. Thinking about it made my head hurt. So instead, I concentrated on today's lesson: Side-passing.

"How about you show me what you've done?" my instructor, Linda, asked. I liked Linda for so many reasons, not the least of which was that she thought Phoenix smelled nice. "It brings back memories of when I was little and of horse camp." God had clearly endowed her with an exceptional sensor.

I showed her what I had been trying, with mixed results at best. I stood at his side, a few feet away, and asked him to alternately cross over his back feet and his front feet to move sideways. There was lots of hand-waving, tapping with my stick, cajoling and commotion on my part. Although there were moments of sheer side-passing brilliance, more often than not we both wound up confused and discouraged.

"Not bad," Linda said, ever the diplomat. "He definitely has the idea. But how about I show you a slightly different approach? It's called 'the windshield wiper'. Can you ask him to stand with his nose facing the wall?"

O.k. Done.

"Now, hold your stick just so," she said, holding the end of the stick near his round tummy and pointing toward his hiney. "Now alternate moving the stick toward the rear end and toward the nose. When you get good at it, and speed it up, the stick resembles a windshield wiper waving back and forth, but without contacting him."

In theory it sounded good, and in practice it was somewhat successful. But as I watched Phoenix, it occurred to me that while his feet were indeed crossing over at times, I wasn't sure he understood why he was moving his feet as he was. He simply seemed to be preoccupied with avoiding the stick rather than with where, exactly, he was placing his feet.

"I don't know, Linda," I said hesitantly. "I mean, I'm a pretty good dancer, but I didn't learn by someone shooing me across the dance floor."

"How about we just give it some time to sink in. Try it, and let me know how it goes."

We ended the lesson with a promise to do just that.

I returned Phoenix to his pasture. Instead of lingering at the gate to watch him roll and shake himself off like a giant dog before ambling slowly away, I hurried home. Jon was coming home today from his trip with Jenna, and I was excited to see him. Really excited, which was both surprising and ... nice, actually. I was reminded of when we lived apart, and how our reunions never disappointed our borderline unrealistic expectations.

The week had flown by quickly. Trips to the barn, two counseling courses with their intense summer schedules, and landscapers swarming the yard like a group of worker bees. The noise and the mess were intense as they broke down and hauled away the old patio.

I heard the garage door open shortly after I finished showering and dressing.

"Hey! Welcome home!" I said, rushing to give him a kiss.

"Hey," he said, giving me a quick peck. "I'm feeling icky from the flight," he said in response to my questioning look. "Just let me get settled." And with that he grabbed his bags and headed straight to the laundry room. In less than two minutes, he had unpacked, closed the lid and started the cycle.

Okaaay... By now, I was used to his OCD-like tendencies, but even this was interesting. *Nevermind. He's back!*

"So...how was it? Was it amazing? I haven't talked to you much since you've been gone. I want to hear all about it!"

"It was great. Beautiful." He headed to the shower, taking his clothes off on the way. I stood outside the shower and continued chatting.

"I can't wait to see some pictures. I got the one that you sent me a few days ago. Did you take one standing next to a tree and looking up? Did you take any of you hugging a tree?"

"Oh, this feels so good," he said. "Airports are the worst." I watched as he stepped out of the shower. My eyes travelled down his body, his muscles strong from years of working out. I never got tired of looking at those muscles.

"Yeah, you look exhausted," I said, teasing. "In fact, you look like you could use a nap right now. In fact, you probably shouldn't even bother getting dressed," I said, running my fingers through his chest hair.

"Nice thought. But I need to go through the mail and see what the landscapers have been up to."

O.k. Don't panic. You know how he is. Just give him some time. He just needs to feel more settled before he can relax.

I continued to tell myself this when he fell asleep early. And all the next day. By Day 3, it was finally beginning to ever-so-slowly-kinda-sorta dawn on me that maaaaybe something was wrong. My first clues were that the laundry was done, the yard was mowed, sleep was caught up on, mail was sorted, the presentation for work was completed, and – thank god - workouts were back on track – chest, legs, abs, and chest again. My second clue was that I had not yet had the pleasure of a proper reunion. My third clue was that I had yet to see anymore pictures.

Ain't nothing gets by me, that's for darn tootin'.

"So…," I finally began, "… is something wrong?"

"No," he said, in a tone that implied "why do you ask?" while continuing to eat his sandwich.

"Well…." I continued, "I get the distinct impression you're avoiding me. And I'd still love to see your pictures."

"Nope. Nothing wrong."

"Okaaay…so there's nothing we need to talk about?"

"Nope."

"Hm." *So why are you being such an obsessive-compulsive douchebag? Oh - so that's what OCD really stands for! At least, in this case. Shine the light.*

At that point, I could have chosen Door #1: Insistence. "Something's clearly wrong, and I'm not leaving until I get some answers from you," followed, if necessary, by my irrefutable evidence of all the things he has found to be more important than me during the past three days.

Or Door #2: Empathy. "Sweetie, I care about you and I want to help. Something's clearly wrong. Can you please share with me what it is?"

Instead, I chose Door #3: The Obvious Choice. The Choice of Champions. I waited until he went for a marathon bathroom session, of which only men are capable, and checked his phone.

When I saw the text message, my heart pounded several times before sinking to my knees and causing them to buckle.

Terri: Hey, I'm outside your meeting now. Got time for me?

Jon: For you, always! Be right out.

O.k. O.k. Stay calm. Be cool. Act like you don't know. Think. O.k. I've got it. Bring up Terri's name. Casually, not like you know they met during one of his meetings because you were snooping on his phone. Not like you're envisioning them trying to rip each other's clothes off while lip-locked in the hallway.

Or not.

"So, question for you," I said, bursting into the bathroom. "Are you having an affair?"

"What the...No...No!"

"Oh. Well, so sorry to interrupt." I dropped the phone on the countertop and left. *So sorry to commit shittus-*

interruptus. Please, by all means, carry on, Captain Crap-tastic.

"And thank you VERY much for breaking into my phone!" he yelled as he followed after me, trying in vain to wipe his butt and pull up his sweatpants as he walked. For Jon, the Golden Rule wasn't the one about doing unto others. It was the one about having a good offense.

"Terri is a friend. Nothing more! We happened to be in the same building. Jesus! You broke into my phone? Unbelievable!"

"Then what the HELL is going on?"

Silence.

"Tell. me. What. Is. Going. On." My gaze was unwavering. I didn't need to tell him that I wasn't leaving until I got some answers.

More silence was met with more unwavering gaze.

"You were rude to me," he said finally, softly.

"Rude to you?"

"When I called you from the hotel. Early on in the trip. You were so rude."

"When did...what the ..." I stammered, my mind racing. "You mean the first time we spoke? After playing phone tag for two days?"

"Yes. That one. You practically hung up on me," he said, doing an exaggerated, sarcastic-yet-passable imitation of me saying "Fine. Don't worry about it. We'll talk later."

"Are you serious? You've barely spoken to me for three days because I was rude to you? Yeah, I probably was rude to you. We hadn't connected for two days. I had landscapers here asking me questions that I don't know the answer to. I came home late after two classes and a midterm exam. I'm missing you, and finally able to talk to you, and you tell me you only have a few minutes, that you have to head out to dinner. I'm sorry if I was rude. Really, I am. But does that mean I deserve … this?"

My mind was still desperately racing back in time. I paused as a sudden realization hit me. "Wait. We talked several times after that. Why didn't you mention it? I had no idea."

"No, *you* have no idea. It put a damper on the whole rest of the trip." More silence. And then, "I'm done."

"What do you mean, 'you're done'?" I ask.

"I'm done. Through."

Once again, Jon was telling me he wanted a divorce. Un–be-lievable.

This time, however, I did not cry. I did not panic. I did not beg, guilt-trip, or crumble. I had no urge to run or to disappear. Of course, this could have been because after three other "I want a divorce" declarations over the course of as many years, I'd had a lot of practice. But now, I simply had two near-simultaneous thoughts go through my head:

This is not about me.

I do not deserve this.

Oh my gosh. I think I HAVE been plunged! EMDR rocks!

With those thoughts, and the support of my newly-formed spine, I said simply, "O.k." as I turned and calmly walked away.

That would be the beginning of the end of the worst years of my life.

I didn't know that at the time, though. I was still too stunned to know anything. So I did the only thing that seemed to make sense: I went to see Phoenix.

I stood in the empty arena with him, not quite sure exactly what we would do. It was hot – too hot to even contemplate putting a saddle on him. I groomed him slowly, thoughtfully, running the brush down his strong neck, across his back, softly along his flank, flicking away the dirt and dust at the end of each stroke, all the while talking, rambling, softly.

"Things pretty much suck right now, buddy. Not gonna lie to you. I'm up that proverbial creek big-time. I have no idea what I'm going to do."

I paused and thought for a moment. "But I guess it's really no different than what horses deal with all the time, is it? You're dependent upon some volatile person who can change their mind at the drop of a hat. You're never quite sure which version of them is going to show up on any given day. You try to tell them, try to communicate, but they don't hear you. So you tell them again, maybe with a kick, a bite, or a buck, and that's it. Someone gets hurt. 'That's unacceptable. I'm done with you,' they say. And your life is turned upside down. You're put out to pasture, or sold as a problem horse. If you're a dog or a cat, you're taken to the shelter. Or worse. All for committing the egregious sin of trying to tell someone how you feel. Or that you're hurting."

No wonder women and horses share a bond.

I looked up to find his head turned slightly. He was looking directly at me, his soft brown eyes holding my gaze. Those eyes seemed to reach down to infinity.

"What? Am I right or am I right?"

He swung his head back, licking his lips in a sign of relaxation. I continued to stare at him, thoughts swirling, my mind's eye blinking in the bright light that was starting to shine.

"You and I aren't so different after all, are we? You tried to tell me, didn't you? You tried to tell me that you weren't ready for such a long trailer ride. That your feet were hurting afterwards. That the farrier wasn't such a good idea just then. And I didn't listen, did I?"

We stood together for some time, his rear leg cocked in relaxation. My arms were draped over his back where a tear fell on his brown and white spots. "O.k.," I said finally. "How about we start over?" I led him to the middle of the empty arena, and stood in front of him.

I addressed him formally and softly.

"Phoenix. I would like you to side-pass. I would like you to cross your front and back feet over each other as you move to the side. I know this might seem silly to you, but trust me, it will be helpful. I might need you to side-pass up to a gate so we can open it. I might need you to get out of a situation on the trail. So I think it will be helpful for you to learn where your feet are and how to move them more thoughtfully. If it's any consolation, I had to take ballet lessons when I was little. Now I'm no ballerina any more than you're a dressage horse, but it can't hurt for both of us to learn how to move better, right? You with me?"

More licking, and then a big sigh. I scratched his itchy forehead and smoothed his forelock. Then I moved to his side, and placed my hand on his flank, rubbing gently.

Feel this? Feel my finger, as light as a fly landing on you? Good. Now I need you to move. Take your time. Think about it. I know you know this. Yes. Good. You shifted your weight. Good job. More rubbing. *That's it. Now feel my finger on your neck? Yup. That's it. Now I need you to move your front feet. Take your time. Tiny step. Perfect. Stop for a minute. Think about that.*

His eyes were staring into space. *Wait. Just wait.*

"Where are you? Where did you go to, Buddy?" More rubbing. Finally, blinking and licking.

You back? Ready to try again? Good! Feel my finger on your side? Tiny step. Very good! Take your time. Think about where your feet are. We're in no hurry. Good. Hold your head just so – that will make it easier. And it makes you look very handsome. O.k…try once more…but this time, let's move both your front and your back feet….

I'm not a trainer. I don't claim to know a lot about horses. But I had forgotten one thing: I know THIS horse. I know this horse because I know myself. And right now, for better or for worse, I was his best shot.

This was going to be a long road. Sometimes, as Linda said, you just have to get back to zero, to where you were before things went south. Phoenix and I both had to get back to our zero. And we would get there together.

MORAL OF THE STORY SEVEN: STAY IN GRATITUDE

Sometimes things just have to suck for a while until they get back to zero. There's no way around it, and not much you or anyone can do to make things better. Death, divorce, illness, injury - so many bad things can happen that will just take time to heal. And yet, living with uncertainty and uncomfortable feelings is really hard, especially for control-freak conflict-avoiders like myself. I want everything to be o.k, to be my way, and, like the annoying, spoiled kid in Willy Wonka and the Chocolate Factory, I want it NOW.

Keeping in mind that alcohol, ice cream, and binge-watching stupid shows all are valid options, I found I have a patent-worthy process for dealing with challenging times. It passed the acid-test of one of the worst weeks of my life: The Infamous Week-Before-Christmas.

I had only recently started my new job, and was still in the stressful trying-to-remember-names stage. In a single week, I had three final exams, and had to finish packing before the movers came to move me out of Jon's house. In the midst of all this, my beloved dog suddenly took ill. On moving day, I took her for her final vet visit. I was all alone for Christmas, and too shell-shocked to care.

First, I continually reminded myself that it's o.k. to not have all the answers. Or even any of them. Because, actually, we don't really know much of anything - we just think we do. You might think your world has fallen apart, but all that's really happened is you have just been rudely reminded that we were never guaranteed our world was together in the first place.

I kept repeating to myself: "I don't know and that's o.k. Right now, my only job is to handle this day/this hour/this task/this next breath." My simple rule of thumb is, the more things suck, the closer I bring in the horizon.

Second, I did my best – my absolute best – to stay in gratitude.

Seriously? That's all you got? "Everything will be o.k. and be glad things aren't worse?"

Yeah, pretty much. Well, no, actually, there's more, but these are the basics. And they're really powerful.

As a prone-to-depression pessimist for much of my life, living in gratitude was something I had to learn verrrry slowly, and with a lot of repetition. I had to purposefully counter each negative thought with a Pollyanna-like "but, at least…" When I wake up, instead of cursing the alarm and dreading facing a chilly room and being bummed I have to go to work, I am grateful for my warm bed, for my furnace that will kick on soon, and for the fact that I have a job to go to. It may sound like the stupidest cliché of all time, but you have to remember that things could almost always be worse. Literally. I reminded myself of this even if I had to do it through clenched teeth or while rolling my eyes. Now, I don't have to consciously practice it so much, and the phrase "it beats the alternative" is more just a part of my being.

But how can we be grateful for the really bad things that happen? For those things that turn our lives upside down, or are so gut-wrenchingly unfair or awful?

Remember when I said that we are not alone, and that we are part of a team? I now absolutely believe that we chose this life and the lessons we wanted to learn. Sometimes we learn them easily, sometimes we have to be hit over the head. Maybe, like me, even multiple times. And since we chose these lessons, I'm grateful for the opportunity to finally learn them. Maybe I'm being given the opportunity to right some wrongs, some of which may not even have happened during this lifetime, or which have been going on for generations.

And we do have choices in how to respond to a situation. Choices in what to focus on, what to ignore, what to believe, how to respond, and even in what to feel. For me, choosing to live in gratitude has been life-changing.

In one of my favorite series, *"Call the Midwife,"* Nurse Lee was questioning how God could let something so awful happen, and in the process, was questioning her faith. Sister Julienne, trying to offer comfort, said that God never gives us more than we can handle.

"Forgive me, Sister," Nurse Lee said flatly, "but I don't see how God enters into any of this."

"My dear," Sister Julienne replies, "God isn't in the act. He is in our response to the act."

Chapter 8

Into the Mist

"Just keep swimming…just keep swimming…."

~ From the movie *Finding Nemo*

"So where are we going today?" Diana asked. She wasn't asking in the literal sense - we weren't sitting in a car or wandering around a shopping mall. We were speaking on the phone, and she was asking what area of my life I wanted her to look at during her psychic reading.

"I just need to know one thing," I said. "Is the universe totally fucking with me?"

"Excuse me?" she asked, a bit surprised.

"Did my guides wake up one morning and think, 'You know, this love and light is all well and good, but it's getting a little boring. We need some entertainment. Ooh! I know! Let's mess with her. Just for giggles.' You know, like some sort of cosmic April Fool's Day."

"Well, that would be the first I've heard of such a holiday," Diana replied. "But why don't you fill me in a little bit."

"Well, despite the situation with Jon, and the fact that most every aspect of my life is up in the air right now, I was actually doing well. Things were finally, finally coming together in the most amazing way. I was so excited."

"Like what things?" Diana asked.

"Well, you know I have desperately been trying to find a job in New Mexico, so I could move back there."

"Yes."

"A job finally opened up, and I had a phone interview. Now, I'm not the greatest at phone interviews, but this one went really well. We talked for over an hour. At the end of our conversation, I mentioned that I happened to be planning a trip to New Mexico in a couple of weeks, and would be happy to meet with her in person. She was really excited about that, and we scheduled the interview."

"Did you actually have it? How did it go?"

"I did, and it went wonderfully. Not only that, but so many things fell into place. One of my best friends happened to be out walking her dog when she struck up a conversation with a neighbor. She was getting her house ready to sell, and it was just around the corner of my friend's home. It was beautiful – perfect for just one person. She wouldn't be ready to move for a few months, but – get this – the house right next door was available, and the owners agreed to a short-term lease. The house was also within a few minutes' walk from the stable area. There was a stable lot available, right next to that of my good friend, where I could keep my horse. I could even see it from my backyard. We would be barn buddies, able to look out for each other's' horses."

"That all sounds wonderful."

"Couldn't be better! I was on Cloud Nine. When I got home, I ordered moving boxes and looked into horse transport options. I had one foot out the door."

"Had?"

"Had. The day after I returned, I received the call. The woman said simply, 'The position has been filled.' No 'Thank you for coming.' No 'it was a tough decision.' It was so...so...impersonal! My heart sank. I didn't even try to hide my disappointment. Seriously? What. The. Hell. Now I feel so let down. Like all the work you and I have been doing to learn how to tap into my intuition has been for nothing. Like I misread all the signs. Either that, or the universe is fucking with me. I need to know which it is."

"Wow. O.k., I see where you're coming from. Let's see what we can find out." We were both quiet for a moment, until she finally said:

"You had to experience 'flow.'"

"Flow?"

"Flow. You were in a state of flow, when things seem to magically fall into place. You needed to experience that, so you'll recognize when it happens again. And it will happen again. But until then, you're in what I like to call the Irish Mist."

"Irish Mist?" I was beginning to feel like a confused parrot, simply repeating everything she said but with an added question mark.

"It's like when you're in a thick fog, like the kind they get in Ireland." As was her habit, she slipped into a bit of an Irish brogue when she said the last part of the sentence. "So thick you can't see your hand in front of your face. When you're in that situation, you can only see the next step ahead of you, if that. You have to rely on your instincts. You have to trust in that one step you can see, even if you can't see where it leads. The universe isn't messing with you. You weren't misreading the signs. You just had to have this experience."

I thought about this for a moment, as I slowly digested the idea that I had not been the unwitting victim in an episode of Celestial Candid Camera. Apparently, instead, when I chose this life, I had enrolled in AP Experiential Learning.

Honestly, guys – next time just give it to me straight. No need to arrange some elaborate high-hopes goose chase. If you're not sure how to do that, maybe the person who called me with the news about the job can help you out. She seems to have no problem being straightforward.

"I've been in such a mist before," I tell Diana. "But it wasn't Irish. It was Canadian."

It was near Vancouver Island, on a week-long kayaking trip. I was in a group of about ten people, along with two guides. We kayaked during the day and camped in the wilderness at night. Everything we needed – food, drinking water, tents, even a portable toilet – was packed into our kayaks. We were this amazingly self-sufficient intrepid little band of explorers, complete with gourmet meals, a real toilet seat, and the requisite there's-always-one-in-the-group annoying travel companion. And this time, it wasn't me.

Most of the time, we hugged the shoreline, but a day came when we had to do a crossing to another island. It didn't sound like too big of a deal. We were, after all, Intrepid Explorers. Except that morning, a thick fog covered the water.

"No worries," our guides reassured us. "We'll be broadcasting our whereabouts, so they'll know to look out for us."

"They? They who?" I asked. I was envisioning the whales in the area tuned into short-wave radios, all wearing ginormous headphones.

"The ships."

"Oh. O.k. Wait, did you say ships? As in, really big boats?" I asked, feeling my eyes widening as my happy vision of gossipy whales vanished.

"This channel is a shipping corridor. Sometime big ships come through. But don't worry. We'll let them know to watch for us." *Said the rocks along the coastline to the Exxon Valdez.*

As we set out, we could see each other in our group of about 7 kayaks, but not much further. At first it was just eerie. Then it was disconcerting. Then downright nerve-wracking. We paddled and paddled and paddled, but without any landmarks to mark our progress, it felt like we were standing still. Left, right, left, right...I just kept working, sweating, not knowing for certain whether it was having any effect.

Oh my god ... will this never end?

You know, you can whine all you want, but it won't change the fact that paddling on is the only way you're going to get wherever it is you're going. Besides, this whole trip was your idea. You're living the dream, remember?

Oh, shut up, you. I'm not in the mood for Miss Pollyanna Gratitude farting rainbows and unicorns just now. Why don't you just go back to being your nasty, critical inner self?

Eventually, though, I did see the futility of worry and internal whining and hopelessness, and I began to relax. As my anxiety gave way to curiosity, I realized there was quite a bit to see. Occasionally, a fish would disturb the quiet water, or a sea lion would pop its head above the surface, bobbing quietly as it watched us go by. I imagined a Far Side cartoon in which he went home to his family, and as his sea lion wife wearing a flowered dress with her sea lion hair in a perfect coif took his coat and briefcase he tells her, "Guess what? I saw a real live human today!"

After what seemed like several hours (though in reality was probably only one), we saw the vague outline of the shore approaching, and knew we had made it. We cheered as if we had just discovered the New World after a month of sailing.

An Irish Mist. What a good description. I still had no job, and no idea how I was going to support myself. And until I knew where I would be working, I couldn't really begin to search for a place to live. And until I could move, I was living with someone for whom my very presence was as irritating and uncomfortable as a pebble – no, never mind a pebble – a giant, jagged rock, in his shoe.

The tension was as thick as that mist that surrounded our little kayaks, but without support or broadcasting of any intentions whatsoever. I avoided him, and avoided Jenna during her visits. As much as I missed her, I just didn't have the energy to put on the required good face or to endure Jon's inevitable wrath if I didn't.

If my past behavior was any indication, I should have been panicked and hopeless during this time. My well-honed flight instinct should have kicked in, urging me to damn the torpedoes and simply pack up and leave. And yet, I was strangely calm. I had the oddest, most uncharacteristic feeling – despite all evidence to the contrary - that everything would be o.k. I could present no supporting evidence whatsoever for this hypothesis. I knew that on paper things did not look good.

Gratitude. Stay in gratitude. Things could be worse, right? Things are uncomfortable, but at least I don't have to be afraid of Jon. He's pushy and overbearing and has to have everything his way, but least he's not deliberately being an asshole. I have no job or income of my own, but at least I have a roof over my head while I figure it out. I have no idea where I'll live, but least now I'll be able to find a place that feels like home. At least I have an education, a profession. At least I have family and friends, even if they're not close by. At least I have my horse, who's starting to like me again. At least...at least...

The call came shortly after my session with Diana. Could I come for a second interview? Even as I said yes, of course, my mind raced to place the company. I had applied at so many places. Oh, yes. That one. I had interviewed over a month ago, and heard nothing. I'd written it off, chalked it up to yet another cold, unfeeling Corporation in complete control of the multitude of pitiful job seekers. Which was a shame, I thought, because it sounded like the perfect job.

As I would find out, it was the perfect job. The shoreline had suddenly become visible through the mist. I had made it. Unfortunately, the shoreline had turned out to be Indiana, not New Mexico. This Midwestern shoreline – this place where I continued to feel so desperately lonely - would have to do for now. But inside, I still cheered as if I had reached the New World.

Another call came a few months later, from a friend in New Mexico.

"Remember that job you applied for?" she asked, barely concealing the excitement in her voice.

"How can I forget?"

"Be glad you didn't take it. The company has wound up in some legal difficulties. People are getting laid off. You dodged a bullet."

Wow. O.k. I know I should stay in gratitude and all that, and feel badly for the employees who are the unwitting victims of the bad choices of management. And I do feel bad for them. Really. But...oh, screw it...

YESSS!!! SUCK IT, LITTLE MISS 'THE POSITION'S BEEN FILLED'!!!

MORAL OF THE STORY EIGHT: TRUST

I didn't know at the time I was paddling through the Canadian Mist that I was experiencing what later would be such a valuable lesson. And such a difficult one.

Trust continues to be my biggest challenge. No matter how many times my prayers have been answered, no matter how many bullets I dodge, no matter how many amazing "unexplainable" experiences I have, my skeptical left brain still tends to first turn to doubt, to seek a rational explanation. "Are you sure?" I continually find myself asking my guides. "That doesn't sound right." And that's o.k. Questioning is allowed. But in return, apparently those whom I'm questioning occasionally get to have some fun in the form of their own version of a goofy tv reality show. After all, fair is fair.

Like our kayaking guides, our spirit guides are looking out for us. They can see where we are headed even if we can't, and their job is to act in our best interest. But it doesn't mean we should just sit back and wait for things to happen, or be stupid about things. We still have our job to do of navigating the human world, and we should be broadcasting our intentions and wearing our life jackets as we do so.

The Wiccans (and probably other traditions too) have a saying for this, which is to "act in accord." Meaning, we can ask for what we want, but then we must do everything reasonably in our power to help our case. If there comes a point when you've done everything within your power, your situation still hasn't resolved and you're still paddling blindly, then you face a choice: You can be miserable and fight and whine about the unfairness of it all, or accept your circumstances.

Our culture values self-reliance and self-control. Acceptance is sometimes viewed as weakness. To me, however, acceptance doesn't mean you're giving up. On the contrary. Acceptance is about taking back your power. Instead of wasting energy on anger, blame, and resentment, you can choose to trust that there is some higher reason for the situation. So, you might as well relax and enjoy the proverbial sea lions that pop their heads up above the water.

Chapter 9

RBI's

*If you think to ask the question, you might be surprised
at the answer you get.*

~Juli Piovesan

"Sorry. I know the answer to that, but it's escaped me. I'm having a bit of an introvert moment. I'll get it to you later."

I nodded without looking up, and continued making notes as I went about the process of taking my co-worker's invention and translating it into the sleep-inducing legalese of a patent application, so indecipherable that it would essentially render the idea unrecognizable to all but the nerdiest of the nerds: "In one embodiment, the present invention comprises a polyolefinic, non-breathable film laminated to substrate, said substrate comprising co-located apertures in register with a water-insoluble ink."

Oh, good lord, it's a panty liner. And it's got pretty pictures on it, probably of flowers and dancing women having happy periods. Why can't we just say that? Suddenly, I stopped and looked up, confused.

"What do you mean, an 'introvert moment'?" I asked. "Don't you mean a 'senior moment'?"

"No, I mean an introvert moment. And excuse me? Are you calling me old?" he asked, laughing.

"Pffft…" I said, with a dismissive wave of my hand. "Calm down. I'm just calling you a liar is all."

Now it was my turn to laugh. After all, I wasn't sure I wanted to live in a world where you can't have fun while discussing panty liners in great, glorious detail.

"But what do you mean, an introvert?" I continued. "Introvert my hiney. You're not an introvert."

"Actually, I am. And I just read an eye-opener of a book about it. I'll lend it to you if you're interested."

More than once, when I confessed my introversion, people have reacted with the same amount of surprise as I just did. Most people saw my fun, outgoing side, which could at times make me seem downright extroverted. But I knew the truth. Social gatherings with people I didn't know well were something I braved. The term "networking" could just as well be the title of a horror movie.

I had also confirmed my introversion with the Myers-Briggs personality test (a solid ISFJ), as well as numerous waiting room magazine quizzes. However, Marti Olsen Laney's book, "The Introvert Advantage," would show me that what I didn't know was a lot. Reading it was one continuous, bona fide "Oprah A-Ha Moment."

First, I didn't know how much of an introvert I was. I passed the quiz in Chapter 1 with flying colors, scoring 24 out of 29, which is, according to Laney "pretty darn introverted." To me, however, it was just disturbing. Extroversion = good, introversion = bad, right? All the world loves an extrovert. They're the fun ones. Introverts are the weirdoes who skulk around the walls during high school dances, and who, as adults, don't even go to the dances.

I also didn't know that there are actual biochemical and physiological differences between introverts and extroverts. That our brains are literally wired differently, and that we store memories differently, in a way that makes them harder to retrieve. This explains why introverts have more so-called "senior moments." If our memories were like cars, extroverts could simply park it in the garage, and pull it out whenever they need it. As I understand it, with introverts, it's as if before pulling the car out of the garage, we first have to grab the steering wheel from the bedroom, the gas pedal from the bathroom, the keys from our coat pocket, and the wheels from various places out in the yard.

I didn't know that my frequent inability to remember names – including of people I've known for years – is a trait of introverts. Or the tendency to not think well under pressure. Or to dread phone calls. Or to need time to process information. Or to be misunderstood by others and regarded as aloof. Introversion was so much more than dreading parties.

By the time I finished the book, I would not only be o.k. with being an introvert, but would be downright proud of it. Because, as it turns out, we also have a lot of gifts. We are the deep thinkers. The patient ones who can stick with difficult and complex tasks until they are completed. We are the planners, the listeners. Without introverts to question the extroverts and rein them in a bit, they would just constantly be off flitting from one grandiose idea and social gathering to the next. We, however, are the few, the proud, the party-poopers.

But my enlightenment and relief soon gave way to anger.

Why didn't anyone tell me this? I spent my entire life beating up on myself for not being able to be like others. Why couldn't I just be normal? Why can't I just get along with people? All this time, I thought I was just weird. Now I find out there's nothing wrong with me. Well, at least not that. There might be plenty of other things wrong with me, but not this. And I'm not alone. But it explains why I often feel so different and alone. My siblings? Extroverts. The other women on the trip to Michigan? Extroverts. Most attorneys? Extroverts. Dammit! Why did I have to wait until now to figure this out?!

As it turns out, the rule of like attracting like applies to introverts. Several of my closest friends are introverts. Jon is one as well – perhaps even more pretty darn introverted than me. Even more important, so is my horse.

As Pat and Linda Parelli explain, horses also come in basic personality (or as they call it, "horsenality") types. Like people, they can be introverts or extroverts. And because horses are prey animals and have highly developed survival instincts, they can also be predominantly right-brained or left-brained. Phoenix is a right-brained introvert, or RBI. And like me, he scores pretty high on the introversion scale. The freezing, the lights-are-on-but-nobody's-home look, needing lots of time to learn new things, his non-demonstrative and reserved demeanor – easily misinterpreted as simply obedient - all were actually clear signs of an RBI.

If Phoenix were to even go to his high school dance, he would be sitting in a corner playing games on his horsey iPhone the entire time.

I continued to process my newfound insights about what it means to be an introvert during my next visit with him. We were taking a break from our umpteenth trailer loading session, and he grazed nearby as I perched on a flatbed trailer, sipping a diet soda. I had jettisoned the idea of my happy trail riding season in favor of addressing the root of his issue. I had vowed that I would do whatever it took, not just to get him loading easily, but to help him be so comfortable with it that it would be his idea to go in.

This was proving easier said than done. After several weeks of training sessions in which we edged closer to trailer, I had finally convinced him to put his nose inside before snorting and prancing away. After a few more sessions, I had convinced him to put his head inside, then one foot, and then to stand with both his front feet inside. No amount of patient encouragement, however, would convince him to go all the way in.

I had been told by trainers in the past that I need to "commit" to his going in. To stand at the side and give clear signals, using a strong voice and swinging my stick and string to encourage him, leaving no doubt in my mind or in his as to what the end result would be. *Envision him in the trailer. BE the trailer...* I can allow him to pause and take his time, but under no circumstances should I allow him to refuse, to turn around and walk away. His trailer needed to be his safe place, the only place where he was allowed to rest.

It was a wonderful theory, and had worked well with him in the past.

He was having none of it now.

I continued to ponder and sip. Once again, I wish I smoked. It always seems like people who smoke have deep and brilliant insights while doing so.

Think...think... Phoenix is an introvert. But that's nothing new. "To be regarded by others as aloof and often feel misunderstood." Why does this phrase keep running through my mind? Had I misunderstood him? Even armed with knowledge about working with RBI's, had I misjudged him? What was it that I had read in the book about introverts having a different way of learning and assimilating information? Oh yeah...what works for the majority of the population doesn't necessarily work so well with introvert. So true. Someone may have to explain a concept nine different ways to me before some little thing finally clicks and the tenth way makes sense.

I continued to sit and sip my soda, so lost in thought that I was unaware it had become warm and gone flat.

I noticed he was grazing as if he were starving, and yet, his round tummy betrayed the fact that he is anything but starving. I realized most all horses like to graze, but there was this...this...intensity about it.

This can't be hunger. It's like he's stress-eating. Mindless, get-as-much-in-as-fast-as-you can eating, like I do with M&Ms when I'm stressed. Was grazing for him a form of stress relief?

I had learned that horses tend not to eat when they're stressed, so that didn't make sense.

But if he's pretty darned introverted, like me, and if he stress-eats, like me, what if he learns the same way I do? What if he needs that tenth different explanation? What if everything I had been told, everything that might be a perfectly good approach for most horses, just wasn't right for him?

My soda was long gone before an idea slowly formed. I picked up the lead rope, and asked him to once again face the dark, yawning mouth of the rolling container of death.

"Ok, Buddy. Here's the deal. I'm going to ask you to go in. I need you to do this for me. But not until you're ready. Starting now, you can say no and walk away as many times as you want to. But if you do, don't think you get to go off and enjoy some grass while you think about it. No, there's only one way you get to do that, and that's if you go in. If you go in, the deal is, you can come right back out and graze. What do you say?"

Screw you. And the horse you rode in on. Oh wait. That's me. Forget that last part.

I encouraged him forward, and indicated I wanted him to go in. He immediately placed his front feet inside, standing proudly like the Spotted King of the Trailer that he was. I stood, waiting. One breath. Two breaths. Three breaths. Then I asked him to step in all the way. He backed out.

"Ok, that's fine." He tugged on the lead rope, trying to head toward the grass. "Nope, that's not our deal. Try again."

Once again, he stepped in, stepped out, turned away and tugged to go to the grass, and once again, I reminded him, gently, softly, that that isn't our deal.

"I can stand here all day," I said in mock exasperation. "I got nowhere else to be. And that green grass will only keep on getting greener and looking tastier until you go in."

At this point, I faced what I believe is the hardest decision to make when training an animal: when to back off and when to push. At what point do you say, "trust me, this is for your own good," and force the issue? If a child is standing at the end of the diving board, just on the verge of diving in but afraid to take the plunge, at what point do you finally "help" him into the water? And if you do, does he come up thinking it wasn't as bad as all that, or is he more afraid than ever and never wants to go near a pool again?

After several refusals, I took the risk, and swung the stick and string with more energy … and … he went in.

Whew!

And then he immediately turned around. How he managed to slip his big quarter horse hiney around in that confined space, I'm not entirely sure, but there I was, standing face to face with a very smug looking horse.

Well, a deal is a deal. I'll take it.

Breathe. Wait. Rub. "There! Not so bad, is it?"

Speak for yourself. You're not standing in a stupid trailer.

I then invited him to step out slowly, and pointed him to his favorite grazing spot, where he once again ate like he was starving.

Again and again, he went willingly into the trailer – sometimes after changing his mind a few times, but always eventually deciding on his own to go in. It was so beautiful I nearly cried. And then every time, he immediately turned to face me.

"Phoenix, this is wonderful! But I do need you at some point to face forward. I need to be able to tie you and I'd like to put the divider back in. What do you say?"

Nope.

I looked at his lips pursed tightly together, emphasizing even more the wrinkles on his muzzle. "No? Are you telling me no?"

Nope. Wanna turn around.

Sigh. So, the next time, I got creative and rigged his lead rope through the slats so that he would be prevented from turning around.

Ha! See what you think of that, Mr. Smugface!

I think you overestimate your lead rope.

And with one quick jerk, I was left standing with the lead rope in my hand and staring, not at his pleased-with-himself face, but at his spotted hindquarters as he trotted off. With another sigh, I set off to go get him. I wasn't in a hurry. I knew exactly where he would be. Yup, sure enough. Standing outside his pasture, grazing. This time though, calmly instead of frantically.

I asked Linda about it the next time I saw her. "Can horses ride facing backwards? I mean, I know they can, and I've known some who do, but is it safe?"

"I would bet that a pretty significant percentage of horses would prefer to ride facing backwards. And," she continued, "there's an argument to be made for safety, in that, if you have to brake suddenly, it will be their hindquarters, and not their head, that hits the front of the trailer. And no offense, but that means there's a lot more to cushion the blow."

"None taken. Can't deny it – he does have an impressive, er, cushion. But then why don't they? Why do most horses ride facing forward?"

"I don't think anyone thinks to ask them what they would prefer."

Phoenix, however, had spoken. He had informed me that he preferred to reserve his rights to refuse, to ride backwards, and to have full use of the space in his two-horse trailer. If these rights could be respected, he would, when he was ready and on his own accord, go into the trailer. I just needed to trust him.

When I have an introvert moment – whether it's forgetting someone's name, or feeling overwhelmed or misunderstood, or just wanting to curl up and watch t.v. or read a book on New Year's Eve when the rest of the world is partying – I think of the trailer and Phoenix's lesson. I also have the right to refuse, to ride backwards, and to negotiate a mutually-acceptable compromise. After all, my hiney makes a pretty good cushion too.

MORAL OF THE STORY NINE:
HAVE COMPASSION FOR YOURSELF

One of the five Reiki precepts, which I recite daily, is that I will have compassion for myself and for others. I always thought it was interesting that "for myself" had been included. For others, yes, I got that – that was simply part of being a good person. But why specifically include "for myself?" My Reiki instructor once explained that having compassion for ourselves is actually harder for most people than having compassion for others. I now believe that it's also a prerequisite.

Think about it. The Golden Rule says, "Do unto others as you would have them do unto you." If we don't like ourselves very much, then we would have others doing some not very nice things unto us, would we? And doesn't this then give us a free license to do crappy unto others? If we can't even be kind to ourselves, how can we be kind to others? And yet, being kind to others without extending the same courtesy to myself is exactly what I had been trying to do. Often unsuccessfully, I might add.

Kristin Neff has written an entire book about this subject, which I found very helpful. In "Self-Compassion: The Proven Power of Being Kind to Yourself," she explains why this is so important, and also clarifies something I really struggled with. Namely, how is self-compassion different than self-indulgence? If we have compassion for ourselves, and "go easy" on ourselves, aren't we simply excusing a lot of bad behavior?

No. As Dr. Neff explains, self-compassion is about acting in our best interests. When we love ourselves enough to be compassionate to ourselves, we do what's in our best interest, in our highest good. So while it may be in our best interest to occasionally allow ourselves the luxury of skipping a workout when our bodies are tired, or having a hot fudge brownie sundae when we want to reward ourselves, it would not be in our best interest to do that too often, because our health is also important to our well-being.

In order to have compassion for ourselves, I believe we need to understand ourselves. By understanding what being an introvert entails, for example, I could be less hard on myself. It doesn't mean that I decide "well, since I'm an introvert, I should never have to go to a party," or "hey, manners schmanners – I'm an introvert. I'm not so good with people, so deal with it." It does mean that when I am at a social gathering and find myself feeling uncomfortable or out of place, I can talk gently to myself, remind myself that this is normal, that at least 25% of the other people there feel the same way, and that it's o.k. to leave early. And then, I can reward myself for being so brave. Like with a hot fudge brownie sundae.

There's another tool to better understanding ourselves that I found very helpful, though this one is a bit more "out there." I was very skeptical, and normally would not have considered reading the book. But when a good friend whose judgment I trust told me how helpful "The Healing Code," by Alexander Loyd and Ben Johnson, was to her, I took her advice to overlook the style of communication and give it a try. The result was a huge leap forward in my healing process.

The Healing Code itself is a series of hand positions that direct energy to healing centers in our bodies (this is where my Moral of the Story 2 – and another flying leap of faith - comes in really handy), and allows us to focus this healing on specific issues. The challenge is to identify what those issues are, so we can more effectively direct our intentions.

The authors offer a way of helping us identify where our emotional weak spots are. This is done by way of online quizzes that are free and accessible on their website. The Relationship Issues Finder, The Success Issues Finder, The Heart Issues Finder, etc. are all similar, and will generally produce similar results. What they do is help to identify "wrong ideas" that we've somehow gotten in our heads. These ideas can be so ingrained, so much a part of our being, that we're not even necessarily aware of them.

In my case, for example, I found I needed the most help in the areas of Love and Forgiveness, which was not surprising. However, I also uncovered a lot of unproductive beliefs surrounding shame and humility. The authors' explanation of "humility," for example, was especially interesting:

> We believe that humility is one of the most misunderstood things in life. We tend to think that it's someone who always has their head bowed down, who doesn't stick up for themselves. We do not believe that's what humility is. ... Humility means that I believe exactly the truth about who I am. I'm not better than anybody else. I'm not worse than anybody else.

As an experiment, I committed to practicing a Healing Code three times per day, as recommended, for a period of one month. I found the positive changes in me after this time to be clear enough to continue the practice for nearly a year, albeit with the frequency reduced to once a day. The result has been transformative.

By uncovering and healing so many unhelpful and untrue beliefs, I was able to understand myself even better. And in understanding myself better, I was able to have more compassion for myself. And finally, for the first time in my life, I was able to look at myself in the mirror and really love what I saw. NOW I was ready to maybe consider that part about having compassion for others.

Chapter 10

The Transitive Property

Allison: You do everything everybody ever tells you to do, that is a problem!

Andrew: Okay, fine...but I didn't dump my purse out on the couch and invite people into my problems...Did I? So what's wrong? What is it? Is it bad? Real bad? Parents? ... What do they do to you?

Allison: They ignore me.

~ From "The Breakfast Club"

"Will you be able to make me quack like a duck, or walk like a chicken?" I asked suspiciously.

"No. Well, quack like a chicken, maybe, but definitely not those other two."

"How will I know? Will I be aware of what's going on? Will I remember everything, or will it be like waking up from anesthesia?"

"No, it's not like that. It's more like a meditation. You'll be fully aware of your surroundings the whole time, and in complete control. Well, maybe not complete. I guess you could burp. Or fart. Or your eye might start twitching uncontrollably. And if you do, I promise not to post it on Facebook. "

"If it's like a meditation, then how will I know whether the information is real? How will I know that I'm not just making things up, or imagining things? I do that, you know.

I make stuff up and then throw little hissy fits in my head when things don't happen like I think they should."

"Usually, you'll know. Information that's correct will have a certain ... feel ... to it. But not always. Sometimes even verified information simply feels like someone's imagination at the time."

"Have you had clients actually later find corroborating evidence?"

"Sometimes. One client received such detailed information that she was able to identify where and when she had lived. At the time, she didn't believe it. Said it just felt like her imagination. However, she did some digging and found that such a person actually lived. She even located the headstone."

"Wow. That raises a whole new set of legal issues. Like, could she inherit from herself? No wonder reincarnation is poo-pooed. It's just another vast right-wing conspiracy funded by lawyers, right?"

Kathy laughed out loud, then snorted from laughing too hard, which made her laugh harder. This was why I liked her. She not only appreciated my off-beat humor, but wasn't afraid to give it to me straight. She was kind of a rebel in the field of counseling, which was what drew me to her. I knew just enough about the traditional rules of clinical counseling to know that she regularly bent them during the course of our sessions together. The fact that she was also trained in past life regressions was icing on the cake.

"So if past life regressions are real, then why do so many people claim to be Cleopatra? Or Napoleon? I mean, they can't all be, right?"

"Or Marie Antoinette. No, they can't all be. But I often find that if people experience that they were a famous historical figure, often it's not so much literally the case, as that they identify with what that figure stood for. It's more of a metaphor. Something about what that person stood for that they identify with."

"Like being short and needing to have your orders followed without question?"

"Oh, you'd be surprised," Kathy said, rolling her eyes.

Of all the batcrap crazy things you've done, girl, this ranks right up there. A few years ago, you didn't even believe in past lives. Now you're actually trying to visit yours. Well, I'd been looking at crazy in the rearview mirror for quite a while now. I've waved that ship off to sea. A little late to start being concerned with that now.

"O.k." I said, nodding resolutely. "How do we start?"

"I'll guide you through the meditation. If for any reason either of us feels the need to stop, we just stop. Afterwards, we'll take some time to process the information." One more pause, this time as she looked at me expectantly. "Ready?" I nodded.

It started like any number of meditations: Imagine I was in a beautiful place, blah, blah, peaceful, blah, blah, blah. Yeah, yeah, got it. Waterfalls and friendly deer and unicorns everywhere. Then it got more interesting.

"Now you see a set of stairs. There are ten steps. You are going to go down each stair as I count backward from ten. Ten…Nine…Eight…." Down the stairs I went. "Now you see a door in front of you. Take a moment to look at the door."

I imagined a big beautiful door. It was hardwood, like teak or mahogany. It had lots of intricate carving, and gleaming brass handles. *Wait a minute…am I channeling an* Indiana Jones *movie? Never mind. Just go with it.*

"You go to the door and open it. You find that it opens easily. As it swings open, you step through, and find yourself in a mist. You can't see much of anything."

No problem. As it turns out, I'm very at home in mists. Irish, Canadian, you name it.

"Gradually the mist clears, and you begin to look around. Look down at your hands. Look at what you're wearing. What do you see?"

This is absolutely ridiculous. There's no way I'll be able to...oh...wait. My hands are dark-skinned. I'm wearing some kind of leather dress. Moccasins. I'm a Native American woman. Cool!

"As the mist continues to clear, you look around. What do you see?"

I'm in some kind of dwelling. A hut. I'm hiding. There's lots of commotion outside. Like a war, or a raid – there's some kind of enemy. I'm afraid.

"What year is it?"

Somewhere around 1850. How do I know that?

"Look around. What else do you see?"

I peek out a small window and see a man. He's walking right into a trap – I can see the enemy, but he can't. I start to shout, to warn him. But I have children with me. If I shout, I'll give us away. I don't help him. I'm looking for a place to hide in our little hut as I gather my children close to me. Then the images start to fade away.

After Kathy finishes the meditation, and I'm "back in the room," so to speak, I tell her what I saw. "The man – it was Jon. I mean, I'm not sure he was my husband at the time, but I just somehow knew it was my Jon. I felt it. Does that mean we've known each other before?"

"Well, it could. If someone plays a significant role in our life, like he did, chances are we entered into a soul pact with that person. You may have had many lives together."

"Well it's ironic, isn't it? Apparently I couldn't communicate with him then, either." I smiled wryly at the thought. "Do you think we had some score to settle in this life?"

"Usually there's something you need to learn from each other, or some issue you have to resolve. I believe, based on my work, that if you don't resolve it, you'll keep coming back into each other's lives and keep trying until you get it right."

"Well, I clearly had some important lessons to learn from him this time around. And I never would have learned them if it hadn't been for all the struggles we had. So in a sense, I'm grateful to him."

"Recovering from abuse is one of the toughest paths any of us follow."

I continued to be lost in my memories for a moment until it dawned on me what Kathy was saying. "Abuse?" I looked at her with a mixture of shock and confusion. "Whoa. What's with the a-bomb? I didn't really suffer abuse. I mean, as we've talked about a lot, I put up with way more than I should have. But I wasn't abused. I've never been hit in my life. My father never laid a hand on me. Neither did my mother. Neither did Jon. In fact, he spoiled me. Nice cars, amazing vacations, jewelry, dinners – you name it. How is that abuse?"

"Oh, so abuse is income-dependent?" she said sarcastically, giving me a look that said *you know that I know that you know better*. It was another un-counselor-like moment. I got it. "And there are different kinds of abuse," she continued. "Physical is just one kind. Emotional abuse is a real thing."

"I know it exists, but honestly, to me, that seems like just another one of those pop-psychology terms. Or a catch-all. Kind of like in law, when you can't prove negligence, you can always fall back on intentional infliction of emotional distress. Which to me is really just another term for 'he hurt my wittle feewings.' And anyway, like we talked about, Jon may have done and said many unkind things, but he never intentionally set out to hurt me. He just didn't know better. He missed a lot of the same memos I did about communication."

"Like your mom, right?"

"Exactly. She was a good person. I know she loved me. She would never have intentionally done anything to harm me."

I thought of my mother. An alcoholic, volatile husband, and eight children, the youngest ones still living at home. Then at my age suddenly faced with having to find a job with little work experience or training. Talk about terrifying. Talk about hopeless. My situation was a walk in the park compared to what she had to face. And yet, she had done it. I had an enormous amount of respect for her. Sadly, I was too angry to understand this before it was too late.

"So, according to your reasoning," Kathy continued relentlessly, "in order to qualify as abuse, there has to be an element of intent."

"What, suddenly everyone's a lawyer?" I asked in mock-exasperation. "Yes, there does. No. Wait... I don't know. Maybe that's the issue. Maybe we're just not agreeing on the definition. What IS emotional abuse exactly? What's the line between an abuser and someone who's just kind of an asshole at times?"

"Fair enough. How about we look it up? Agree?" She rose, and reached for a book on her shelf, turning to look at me before opening it, waiting for my permission.

"I know what you're doing. You're falling back on the negotiation tactic of agreeing to abide by a neutral reference. O.k. I'll agree. But which book are you using?"

She handed it to me. "The Emotionally Abused Woman," by Beverly Engel. I handed it back to her. "Well, how convenient that you just happen to have it handy," I said.

"I'm going to read a checklist. As I read it, think about Jon and answer yes or no. And you don't have to answer out loud. Ready?"

Again, I nodded.

"An emotional abuser needs to be in control of the situation and the relationship…"

Well, I was the one who had to move if we wanted to be together. And he was the one to decide when and how every relationship he's been in is over. Including ours. That's a yes.

"… is unable to see another person's point of view and to empathize with another's feelings."

That's a big fat yes.

"…is a perfectionist."

O.k., so his nickname was Mr. Perfect ….

"…feels he's always right."

Well, yes, but only because he's unable to see another person's point of view. Though in all fairness, his daughter tried to warn me shortly after we met. "He knows everything," she said. "No, really, you think I'm joking, but I'm not. He knows everything."

"…is overly sensitive to criticism."

Oh dear Lord, yes. He certainly had no problem dishing it out, though.

"…Is impatient, irritable and short-tempered."

Well, there was the f-bomb laden rant when he didn't hear the timer to the dryer go off. Then there was always his legendary impatience in traffic. Or most anytime I was driving. So yes, yes and yes.

"… Has unrealistic, unreasonable expectations of others."

Like expecting me to give up my home, friends, job, and name and then be happy all the time and never get upset? That's a yes.

"… Can be extremely distant, cold, and unresponsive, especially when you are not in his "good graces" or when he desires to punish or control you. Is unforgiving and holds grudges."

Wow. I didn't realize Dr. Engle had ever met him.

"I'm going to go on to read a passage for you I've underlined: 'Some controllers punish by being physically or verbally abusive, while others do so by 'teaching you a lesson' - staying out all night, leaving without saying where they are going, having affairs. Still others simply withdraw, refusing to talk to you and ignoring you or pouting." She read that last passage looking at me instead of at the book.

I stared back, unblinking, suddenly unable to speak. I became vaguely aware of fighting back tears that were forming in my eyes.

Kathy let the silence continue to hang in the air for what seemed an eternity. And then she broke another rule of counseling, which was to always let the client be the one to end a silence. "Sometimes, in order to fully heal, you have to put a name to it. You have to call a spade a spade."

I continued to stare. Finally, barely audibly, I said, "But I can't be an abuse victim. I'm too smart to let myself get into a situation like that. I'm not like that. I'm not like them."

"You're not an abuse victim," Kathy said quietly. "You're a survivor. You said that both your mother and Jon and others would shut you out for hours, sometimes days, when you did something to upset them. You have to understand: Silent treatment is in many ways the worst form of abuse. There are no marks, no outward signs of injury. In some twisted way, it seems kind. It's better than hitting or yelling, right? So you can justify it much easier. You can excuse it with 'oh, but they don't mean to.' But to a young child, it's torture. You're completely helpless, and left trying somehow to fix a situation over which you have no control. And if it comes from someone you're dependent upon for your very survival – like you were with Jon - it threatens your entire sense of security. That's huge. That's traumatic. And very difficult to heal. That's why I'm hitting you over the head with it. You cannot, cannot, cannot stay in denial."

Once again, I sat in silence, letting her words sink in as memories flooded my brain. Of watching, listening intently for any sign from my mother that the days of shutting me out would end. Of doing anything to show how good I was being. *Just ignore people when they're mean,* she'd tell me. *They'll come around.* Of begging Jon to talk to me, to please tell me what was wrong. *If I talk to you, I'll yell, so I get quiet.* The images, the words kept coming. But somewhere along the line they changed. Other memories began to surface. Of me and my previous ex-husband. I looked up at Kathy.

"What's going on up there now?" she asked, pointing to her head.

"Read the list again."

After she had finished, I said quietly, with tears streaming freely, "If I think of myself when you read that list, and not Jon, a lot of those things apply to me too. If I accept that this is abuse, then I'm an abuser. The way Jon treated me? I did the same things to him at times. And it's how I behaved toward my ex-husband. He was a sweet, kind man. I was horrible to him sometimes. And I shut people out too. I do this."

"Then let me ask you this: Did you intend to be abusive?"

"No. Never."

"So is intent an element of abuse?"

I hesitated. I hated to admit when logic had won.

"Apparently not."

"No. It's not." She paused, and I could tell she was considering whether to push or to back off. Whether to throw me off the diving board or insist I just get into the damn trailer. In the end, she swung her stick and rope and insisted.

"This is how abuse gets perpetuated, in the earthly sense. Not talking about any soul pacts here. You were trained from a young age to excuse bad behavior. You had to, in order to survive. And then it became so normal you, that you didn't even see it. When people treated you this way, it flew under your radar. And when you got hurt or angry, as we all do, you didn't know any other way to deal with it, and you behaved badly. It doesn't make you a bad person. It also doesn't excuse the bad behavior. Not on your part, not on Jon's, not on your mother's, not on your father's. That part is real, the hurt is real, the effects are real. And before you can change, you have to begin to *see* it. To recognize it. And to learn a whole new way of being in the world."

By now, I was exhausted. It had been a bit of a day. My head was spinning and thoughts were swirling as I struggled to absorb the magnitude of the events of the afternoon. I left with instructions to, for the love of all that is holy, go easy on myself for the rest of the weekend, and to call if I needed to talk further.

"I will," I reassured her.

I wouldn't. I never do. I hated to bother people. Which is why she called me a few days later.

"Just checking in. I know your type. You'll be sitting around with a thousand thoughts in that big brain of yours, wanting to talk, but not wanting to bother me. Am I right?" Kathy said. I could hear the smile in her voice. "How you doing, girl?"

"Yeah, you're right, but I don't know why I would talk to you ever again," I said. "I come to you for a simple past life regression, and look what happened? I leave a mess of an abuse survivor. Apparently you can't do anything right."

"Yeah, I hate it when that happens."

"There's just one thing I'm still struggling with."

"Seriously, just one? O.k. Shoot."

"What's Jon's excuse?"

There was a moment of silence. "I thought we talked about how there aren't any excu...."

"Not excuse," I interrupted sharply. "Reason. I behaved badly at times, in part, because of what I learned or didn't learn growing up. I get that. But what would cause Jon to be the way he was? He had the most normal childhood ever. I was kind of jealous of that. I met his family. His mother is adorable. His father wasn't an alcoholic. I saw where he grew up. Nice house, nice middle class neighborhood. He was a straight-A student, an athlete, good looking. He had it all. Why would someone like that behave like he did?"

"Do you remember the transitive property?"

"You mean from high school geometry? If A=C, and B=C, then A must equal B?"

"Something like that. A is the experience that leads to behavior. C is the resulting behavior. If you and Jon behaved much the same way at times, then it seems likely that much of the same experiences must have happened. A equals B. Get the picture, Madam Pythagoras?"

"I...I...wait...you're saying that Jon had to be treated the same way?"

"I'm saying that people raised with love and acceptance, with validation of feelings, generally don't behave like bullies. People who are secure – not just acting confident, but secure in themselves – don't resort to pouting or guilt trips or bullying to get their way. People don't have such highly developed defense mechanisms unless they've learned they have to constantly defend themselves. Communication, or lack thereof - shutting people out, silent treatment, or simply being unavailable by choosing to be so busy with other things - all have to be learned somewhere. I'm simply suggesting there may be more to the story than you think."

And with that, I suddenly saw things in a new light.

I had let Jon convince me that he was the normal one and I was the messed up one, the angry one, the one with all the issues. Unlike me, he'd done things the right way: gone straight to college and on to a good job where he stayed and had a successful career, raised a family, built a beautiful home. Now, an alternate reality started to dawn on me: He was as messed up as I was.

I suddenly had an image of two magnets, initially drawn together by some invisible, irresistible force, and then becoming oppositely aligned. No matter how hard you try or how close you come, they would always push each other apart.

Our marriage didn't fail because we were so different. It failed because we were so alike.

Despite trying to stay in love and trying to take the high road after our separation, I had remained stuck in resentment and judgment. I talked a good talk, but deep down was resentful that his life went on much the same as it had, while mine was once again turned upside down. Gone was my budding law practice, my plans to become a counselor, as I threw myself into working full-time.

He got to continue in his job, to stay in his home, to move on effortlessly to another relationship.

Forgiveness was a nice concept, but it was just that. A concept. Now, however, I was suddenly overwhelmed with compassion.

What had happened to him? To that little boy? What had happened to make him feel that he has to be perfect to be accepted? What wounds had to lie beneath the surface to cause such exquisite sensitivity to criticism? What had to happen to cause such impenetrable defenses to be built? How bad was it? Was it bad? Real bad?

All of a sudden, staying in love and forgiveness became real. I actually began to feel on a visceral level his pain and frustration. How awful must that have been for him, to think you've finally found the love you've been looking for all your life, only to find that person isn't who you thought? To encourage me to change my entire life to be with him, and then realize it's not what he wants? To be faced with my unhappiness, my unspoken criticism, my silence, and realize there's nothing he could do? To feel that no matter what he did it wasn't enough?

I wasn't excusing him. I was just finally able to let go of the judgment.

As I attempted to put this into words and explain to Kathy about the light bulb going on over my head, she was silent for a moment. Just as I was beginning to wonder whether we'd been disconnected, she spoke.

"A fish who lives his entire life in the ocean doesn't know he's swimming in water," she said.

"I love that. Who said it?"

"Honestly, I don't know, but it sounds like some very wise Chinese person. So, I realize you have no reason to trust me with another regression, but if you are ever brave enough, come by and we'll try again, o.k.?"

And so it was that I sat in her office several weeks later, walking once more down the imaginary flight of stairs while counting backwards from ten, standing in front of the wooden door. And when the mist cleared, I once again looked down to see moccasins. This time, however, I was staring at the hands of a man. My arms were muscled and had hair like a man's.

I understood that I was a warrior, and very skilled with a bow and arrow. I had been called in front of our Chief, who congratulated me on my bravery in battle. As a reward for my bravery, he had a gift for me. A horse was brought out. He was beautiful – proud, spirited. *Phoenix! I somehow knew it was Phoenix!* Instead of paint markings, he had beautiful spots on his hindquarters, like an Appaloosa. I was in awe. I was also very uncomfortable, because I knew I was not a skilled enough rider to handle this horse. However, I also knew it would offend the Chief to refuse, so I humbly accepted his offer.

The next images I received were of a battle. We were facing white soldiers, like Custer's army. I rode my horse, and carried my arrows. As the command was given to charge forward, he reared, and I fell off. As my horse ran away, I did what I did best: I knelt and began shooting arrows.

After the battle was over, I made my way across the field, among the dead and dying, until I found my horse. He had been shot, and lay dying as well. As I knelt beside his head, stroking him, I apologized.

"If I had been a better rider, this wouldn't have happened. I could have protected you."

"No," I understood from him. "If I had been a better horse, you wouldn't have fallen."

Afterwards, once I was back in the room, I tried to tell this to Kathy.

"I can't explain, really. It didn't unfold like I was watching a video. It just sort of...came to me. Like a sudden 'knowing'. Like it kind of all got dumped on me at once, and then sorted itself out as I told you about it. It feels right. But how do I know it's not wishful thinking?"

"Well, my personal test is whether I could have made it up, even if I had tried. Could you?"

"Never in a million. I don't have that active of an imagination."

"The other thing to ask is whether it makes sense. In other words, given your life with Phoenix now, does this fit in?"

"I am learning how to be a better rider with him. And he takes wonderful care of me. I watch him in the pasture, running and bucking and turning on a dime, and I thank him and God above for not doing that while I'm on his back. When I'm riding him, he's a perfect gentleman. So yes, I'd say it makes sense."

"Good. And I wouldn't share this with just anyone, but I know you'll appreciate it. As you were talking, I received a message for you. It was 'you've been together many lifetimes, and will be together many more.'"

"Guess you're stuck with me, Buddy," I said to him, as I lay draped on his back, soaking in the warm sunshine as he inhaled the new spring grass. He sighed, his soft nostrils fluttering in utter contentment. No sound was more beautiful to me, no feeling more right. I hoped that whatever lay ahead in this life or the next, this memory - this moment - would remain etched in my soul.

MORAL OF THE STORY TEN:
PRACTICE COMPASSION FOR OTHERS

"Just for today, I will have compassion for myself and for others." I had finally arrived at the second half of the last Reiki precept.

Just as a prerequisite for having compassion for yourself is to better understand yourself, I believe to have compassion for others, we need to understand their point of view. Better yet, we need to *feel* their point of view. And the prerequisite for that, I realized, is to stop judging.

Which all sounds good in theory, but how does one actually stop judging?

For me, judgment was like the voices in my head - so second-nature, so insidious, that I wasn't even aware I was doing it. Judging others – "that's awful," "that's so stupid," "she's ugly," "why would anyone do/think that?" "idiot" - was how I was raised. I had often looked upon people with contempt. I had difficulty putting myself in another's place. This in turn made it difficult to understand how hurtful my own words and actions could be.

I have found a simple antidote to judgment that was helpful to me. When I catch myself being a "judgmentalist," as I call it, I simply add the words "to me" at the end of the statement.

"Those tattoos look so ugly…to me."

"That dress looks totally unprofessional…to me."

"He's way too closed-minded and conservative…to me."

Did this solve the problem, and suddenly I was overflowing with love for my fellow man?

No. All it does is remind me that I am seeing things from my own perspective, and through my own lens. What is "too something" for me may not be a problem at all for someone else. This, in turn, allows me to look past the outer layer. To remind myself that this is simply the role that this person has chosen for this lifetime. It's who they *appear to be*, not who they *are*. And who they are is simply another soul, trying as best they can to make their way in this world and learn the lessons they're supposed to learn.

I recently had the privilege of seeing a live performance of *The Lion King*. At the end of an amazing show, I rose with the rest of the audience in a heartfelt standing ovation. My hands grew tired of clapping as one by one the cast took their bows: Simba, Nala, Mufasa, Rafiki…and then came Scar. I noticed that I didn't want to applaud Scar. I didn't like Scar. He was a character everyone loved to hate. I realized, of course, that it made no sense not to applaud the actor, and quickly joined the rest of the audience in honoring his performance.

Later it hit me: If I believe all this spiritual journey stuff, then isn't our life just like one big play? If we choose this life while we are in spirit form, and are born into it on this earth, then aren't we like the actors in the play? Our human form - male, female, our physical appearance, our social status, our job – is the character we've chosen to play. Our spirit, soul, whatever you want to call our eternal form, is the actor. And if I can applaud the actor even though I may not like the character, then can't I love the person without judging the role they chose to play?

I may decide that being around a certain person is not good for me. I may even have to take action to protect myself, or decide my life is better without them in it. I no longer – not for one minute - excuse abusive behavior. I think people who commit violent crimes should go to prison. I think some people really do qualify for a Darwin Award.

But if I see people's behavior as separate from their being – if I see them as fellow actors just doing their best to make their way in this life – my view softens, and whatever I decide comes from a place of love rather than judgment. Rather than allowing me to excuse bad behavior, compassion, ironically, is what allows me to hold others responsible. To hold myself responsible. To set boundaries. And ultimately, to forgive.

Epilogue

Adapted from an online discussion with advice columnist Carolyn Hax:

Dear Caroline: My husband wants to separate/divorce because of many issues that we have. He feels they are mostly my fault.

I'm not perfect, but usually I only react badly if he gets angry at something I didn't even register, or if he insists he knows what I mean or how I feel, etc., when I'm saying something else and trying my best to explain.

I have begged him to try couples counseling. I've also apologized and taken all the blame to keep the peace. But I'm tired of being berated for being "disrespectful." When we're not arguing, things are really good. I don't know whether to keep fighting or to simply agree to what he wants and give up.

Caroline, if I may?

Run. Run fast and far, and don't look back. Because I am willing to bet that the only question you will struggle with, as you bask in the lightness of freedom from endless criticism and controlling behavior, is to wonder why you put up with as much as you did for as long as you did.

Ask yourself this very simple question: Why would you want to waste one more minute with someone who doesn't want to be with you?

Remember that each time you allow yourself to take all the blame, each time you allow yourself to be labeled as "disrespectful" or "selfish" or "angry," or as anything other than the beautiful human being you are, a tiny piece of your soul is chipped away until all that's left is an unrecognizable shell of your true self.

I've come to realize that the times I've been labeled as – fill in the blank, your choice - have tended to be by controlling people who aren't getting their way about something. Because people who are able to respect others' feelings and boundaries don't need to resort to name-calling, guilt trips, pouting or silence. This is not bad communication. It's emotional abuse. And it has to end.

So go ahead – give him what he wants. Because this isn't about you. And you don't deserve this.

About the Author

J. Tanner Jones is a practicing patent attorney, and the author of numerous patents and patent publications. This is her first enjoyable publication. Before being turned to the dark side of the law, she earned a B.A. and a Ph.D. in Analytical Chemistry. She continues to indulge her curiosity of the metaphysical, and patiently awaits enlightenment with the same steadfast optimism of Linus in the pumpkin patch.

CPSIA information can be obtained
at www.ICGtesting.com
Printed in the USA
LVOW11s1338170517
534866LV00001B/12/P